Too many of us have the mistaken notion that busyness is related to godliness and that time stewardship is just a way of cramming more busyness into our lives. The Lord is continually teaching me that the proper use of my time is not to *do* more, but to *be* in right relationship with Him and His plan for my life.

THE HURRIER I GO...

Finding Time for the People in Your Life

BONNIE WHEELER

A Division of GL Publications
Ventura, California, U.S.A.

Rights for publishing this book in other languages are contracted by Gospel Literature International foundation (GLINT). GLINT also provides technical help for the adaptation, translation, and publishing of Bible study resources and books in more than 100 languages worldwide. For further information, contact GLINT, Post Office Box 6688, Ventura, California 93006, U.S.A., or the publisher.

Scripture quotations in this publication are taken from the following versions of Scripture:

AMP—Amplified New Testament, © The Lockman Foundation 1954, 1958. Used by permission.
KJV—Authorized King James Version.
NASB—New American Standard Bible. © The Lockman Foundation, 1960, 1962, 1963, 1968, 1971, 1972, 1973, 1975. Used by permission.
NKJV—New King James Version, Holy Bible. Copyright © 1979, 1980, 1982 by Thomas Nelson, Inc., Publishers. Used by permission.
NIV—The New International Version. Holy Bible. Copyright © 1978 by New York International Bible Society. Used by permission.
TLB—The Living Bible, Copyright © 1971 by Tyndale House Publishers, Wheaton, Illinois. Used by permission.

Published by Regal Books
A Division of GL Publications
Ventura, California 93006
Printed in U.S.A.

Library of Congress Cataloging in Publication Data

Wheeler, Bonnie G.
    The hurrier I Go.

    Bibliography: p.
    1. Time management—Religious aspects—Christianity. 2. Women—Conduct of life. I. Title.
BV4598.5.W44   1985   248.8'43   85-1746
ISBN 0-8307-1033-7

The author and publisher have sought to locate and secure permission to reprint copyrighted material in this book. If any such acknowledgments have been inadvertently omitted, the publisher would appreciate receiving the information so that proper credit may be given in future printings.

To
Dennis, Julie, Tim, Robby, Becky and Benji
who have consistently resisted my best efforts at
organizing them.

Contents

Preface

"So teach us to number our days, that we may apply our hearts unto wisdom" (Ps. 90:12, *KJV*).

"If I have to fill out this I might as well write the book myself—anyway, it's all been said before!"

I had eagerly ripped open the envelope, anxious to read and log in another answered questionnaire as I made the preliminary preparations for writing this book. But that unexpected response, so vehemently scrawled across the bottom of an otherwise empty questionnaire, took me by surprise.

Inadvertently I glanced at a shelf packed with many books on the various aspects of time usage. I automatically started questioning myself: Has it all been written before? Is there really a need for another book on time? Is there really a need for *this* book?

I fumbled through my files searching for some answers. I found:

   • Letters and evaluations from the hundreds of women

who have attended my workshops. "I never realized my time belonged to God," "Learning to say no has changed my life!" "Applying the concept of stewardship has totally rearranged my thinking on time";

• Questionnaires from women honestly stating their needs. "I desperately need daily time with God," "How can I get quality time with my husband?" "How can I stop feeling guilty when I spend time on myself?";

• A study by Dr. James Dobson showing fatigue and time pressure to be the major causes of depression in women;

• A study by a woman's magazine saying that women's most common time-wasting mistake is trying to get everything done without a strategy or plan.

The need for this material to be published was reaffirmed for me. Even with the plethora of published books there are still countless unmet needs and unanswered questions regarding time usage. And even fewer women know what the Bible has to say about time usage or the example Jesus set for us in His use of time.

During the first years of our married life I was an average full-time homemaker with a four-bedroom house and three children. Time management was fairly uncomplicated in those days. I *knew* that my days went better when I started them with God and I had a haphazard interest in plans and schedules.

Then the texture of my days changed dramatically with the addition to our family of three children with handicaps and the start of a writing and speaking ministry for me. Suddenly my interest in goals, priorities and schedules was no longer a haphazard option but a necessity for survival. I have learned and practiced these principles of time management and studied their biblical foundation while combining the care of six children, a husband with a chronic illness, a fifteen-room Victorian home (with no outside help and never enough inside help) with writing, speaking and holding a part-time job outside the home.

Before you start picturing a hyperactive superwoman let me assure you that I am definitely the low-energy type. In fact I often find myself agreeing with comic Flip Wilson, "If I had my life to live over again I wouldn't have the energy!"

I think I have heard almost all of the complaints against time management—"It's so–o–o unfeminine," "I already do too much," "It's unchristian to plan ahead," "Sure you're organized—you were born that way!"

Not only are those views off base, but I find that my use of time is not only intricately interwoven with my mental health and stress control, but is a reflection of my walk with the Lord.

Howard Hendricks says, "The older I become in the faith the more impressed I am that the management of my time is the greatest barometer of my control by the Spirit." Ouch!

We each come to Christ in a unique way; our daily walk with Him differs and subsequently our use of time also varies.

Certain time management principles are basic, but their application will be as varied and individualized as our personal walk with the Lord. To cover this diversity I sent out questionnaires to a wide range of women: students, singles, homemakers, career women, working mothers and widows. Their responses will be interspersed throughout the book.

Because we are all so frail in our humanity I draw heavily from the Bible and its infallibility. You'll discover that the lives of Jesus and His friends, Mary and Martha, have much to teach us that is surprisingly relevant 2,000 years later to our "fast lane" lives.

Not only is our Christian walk unique, but it is in a constant state of transition. Just about the time I am in danger of thinking I have *almost* arrived some new dimension is added that makes me start back at square one.

In the six months after I started this book I had two surgeries, had to find alternative placement for our troubled foster child and work my way through the mourning process on that, and start working at a part-time job outside the home. In the midst of that hectic time God was constantly showing and reaffirming to me that His principles of time usage *do work*.

Too many of us have the mistaken notion that busyness is related to godliness and that time stewardship is just a way of cramming more busyness into our lives. The Lord is continually teaching me that the proper use of my time is not to *do* more, but to *be* in right relationship with Him and His plan for my life.

By the wise use of our time we can all accomplish that which we were created for:

> "What then is the chief end of man? Man's chief end is to glorify God and enjoy Him forever."
> —Westminster Larger Catechism
> 1861

Acknowledgments

Thank You, God,

For each of the women who have shared their time needs and successes by participating in the workshops and answering the questionnaires;

For Susan Dunlap, once again, for her perseverance as reader and reactor;

For Nancy Rolen and her timely help in typing the final manuscript;

And for my editors: Jan Rodger for the idea, Laurie Finlayson for her patience and continual affirmation and Joan Bay Klope for her help and insights with the final product.

Part One
Time Stewardship: Christian Women of Today

It was so difficult for Mary to explain to her sister the compulsion she felt to be near Jesus and hear His every word. Her time with Him was like the last day of summer, when you know the sunshine and flowers will soon be gone and you have to savor each fleeting moment. When she tried to explain Martha laughed at her "flowery speech."

Mary's always been so timid and shy, thought Martha. *Where does she get the chutzpah to sit with the men? I'm surprised the Teacher doesn't send her away! What does she want to be—a rabbi?*

Whenever Mary overheard people talking about her, tears would trickle down her cheeks. *In my heart I feel I'm doing the right thing,* she murmured to herself, *but there's no tradition to follow.*

"Her sister Mary sat on the floor, listening to Jesus as he talked" (Luke 10:39, *TLB*).

Martha bustled around. There was so much to do. Jesus was coming for another visit and she wanted everything to be just perfect for this special guest. There was extra food to prepare and she wanted His room to be clean, fresh and welcoming. Martha felt pressured with all she had to do before Jesus arrived.

Martha had not expected help from Lazarus but she did think Mary should be doing more. She hurried through the house for one last check before going to see to the food. *There is so much to do and so little time—it always seems that the hurrier I go . . . "*

"But Martha was the jittery type, and was worrying over the big dinner she was preparing" (Luke 10:40, *TLB*).

Chapter 1
Mary and Martha of the Fast Lane

"A woman who fears the Lord is to be praised"
(Prov. 31:30b, *NIV*).

Who are the Christian women of today? Who are the modern-day Marys and Marthas struggling to apply biblical principles to life in our contemporary fast lane? Who do they look to for role modeling? What sets them apart from their mothers and grandmothers? What sets them apart from their secular counterparts? What challenges and opportunities do they face? And how do these challenges and opportunities differ from any other time in history?

A Look Back

When I was growing up in the 1950s, all women who worked outside the home were the exception. The women who did attend college were often just marking time until the right husband came along. Fathers teased their daughters about sending them on for their "MRS. degrees."

Those women who opted for careers usually went into one of the caring professions (teaching or nursing) that were considered acceptable and feminine.

Homemakers were in. Career women were out.

In a new book, *American Couples,* the authors present a historical perspective that reflects the experiences of both Christian and secular women:

> . . . within the family, the duties, expectations, and position of each member were always clearly understood and unquestioned. This held true even if everyday reality differed in some respects (as it did in most farming families where men and women were likely to share the same chores). In American families the husband was expected to be responsible for the economic support of the household and the wife for all the "interior" considerations, e.g., child rearing, emotional support of the husband, household chores, relations with friends and kin. When the balance between the husband's responsibilities and wife's responsibilities tipped because of illness or economic exigency, it was generally viewed as a temporary departure from the ideal brought on by unavoidable and extraordinary circumstances. The notion of the "good life" was comprised of the hardworking and prosperous husband, the nurturing wife and mother, and the small happy troop of children for whom she cared while preparing them for an independent future of happiness and achievement.[1]

Not too many years ago we were able to draw a simplistic composite of typical secular and Christian women: adoring wives, devoted mothers, full-time homemakers. Women who received emotional support from their mothers and grandmothers modeled their roles after them. There was a basic security in knowing what was expected of you; a security bound in tradition.

Present Day Marys and Marthas

In the 1980s many Christian women are following the path paved by the secular members of their sisterhood. Even the analyses of many secular women can be applied to Christian women today:

"Today, no one can count on anything. Women can no longer count on seeing their men continue on a given career path. Men can no longer count on women's historic commitment to the home. Whatever were the rules, no longer are. In fact no one really knows what the new rules are."[2]

Anne Follis, homemaker's advocate, says, "With the opportunities have come a few extra headaches. The clearly defined rules and limits on women are gone. They have been replaced by all kinds of exciting possibilities, and all kinds of scary risks."[3]

Consequently no single standardized picture completely characterizes both secular women and many Christian women today. They are set apart from the other women in history by the numbers of them working outside the home and those that are divorced.

WHO ARE THE CHRISTIAN WOMEN OF TODAY?

There is no one "typical" role model for us today. The Marys and Marthas of our time fill a multiplicity of roles: they are still adoring wives and devoted mothers, they are single, have decided to remain childless, are full-time homemakers and many are career women.

Susan is nursing her six-month-old son, chasing her three-year-old, helping her father with a Christmas project and doing the church books. Susan has a teaching credential but is currently working 20 hours per week at the library. "It gives me some necessary income and more time with my family than a full-time job would," she explains.

Kathy has three children, helps her husband lead a weekly

Bible study and is thrilled to be a full-time homemaker.

Darlene is single. She works 40 hours a week, writes, counsels and is taking college classes three nights a week.

Allene is a single parent. After a divorce and 20 years of teaching, she went back to school and is now a counselor.

Mae and her husband have opened a small cafe. This long-time and risky dream had been on hold until their youngest child left home.

Joan is 25 years old and has been happily married for more than three years. Although she and her husband look forward to being parents someday they have agreed that Joan should take advantage of her college education and talents by being a career woman during her twenties.

These six women are all "typical" Christian women.

We Are Homemakers

The full-time homemaker is as rare as any other endangered species. Only 16 percent of today's families have the traditional father as breadwinner and mother as full-time homemaker. The majority of today's Christian families are either assisted by or headed by a working woman.

The women who do stay home face new pressures. Where once being a full-time homemaker used to be the ideal, many now feel it has to be justified.

Where once staying home and raising children was considered a lifelong career, now it is often seen as a six-week maternity leave.

With the exodus of mothers from the neighborhood to the job market the full-time homemaker often falls heir to new responsibilities:

"Can you be Room Mother again? All the *other* mothers work."

"Will you watch Susie tomorrow afternoon? She gets out early and since you're going to be home anyway . . . . "

We Are Single

The Christian women of today are single: widowed, divorced or single-by-choice.

One single-by-choice friend complains, "Everyone assumes that because I'm single, I have unlimited time. I'm always hearing, 'Let her do it, she's single.'" Other single Christians complain of mental and physical fatigue and the inability to bus their children to activities due to full-time employment.

We Are Working Mothers

In telling the effect on the family of the high numbers of mothers who are working outside the home, the authors of *American Couples* write:

> . . . this causes a great deal of reorganization of the family. Young children are placed with relatives or in informal child-care environments. Both men and women worry about the quality of care their children are receiving, and husbands often criticize their wives for leaving the children to go to work, or lose respect for themselves for needing their wives' income. The home is empty during the day and many housekeeping chores are not done until after work—if at all. Men and women come home from a workday tired and often under a great deal of stress, and so their interactions with their children are frequently brief and spoiled by less than ideal amounts of energy and patience.[4]

Christian women are still adoring wives and devoted mothers. However, according to the Census Bureau, 26 million[5] of those adoring wives are part of a two-income marriage. In 1982 there were almost 19 million mothers working outside the home. These figures aren't just reflective of secular women. A survey in *Today's Christian Woman* reported that 2/3 of the respondents worked outside the home at least part time.[6]

Experts call the rate at which mothers are going to work outside the home one of the most important social phenomenons of our time.

Women work outside the home for a variety of reasons:

personal fulfillment, service, using God-given talents, paying for children's college expenses, needing extras. However, more and more of us are working for one reason—economic survival.

Our Hollywood image of a working woman is a glamorous person in a tailored suit, briefcase in hand, and fulfillment oozing from her every pore. In actuality she may be working at a job she doesn't like because she has to. Her pores are more apt to be oozing fatigue than fulfillment.

Personal Perspective

When we were first married, Dennis and I planned that I would stay home with the children (we wanted at least four) and Dennis would provide for us.

For the first 15 years of our marriage we lived out that traditional dream. I loved having a spotless home and well-cooked meals. I made our clothes, baked our bread and did needlework. We eventually parented six children.

In 1977 I started writing during the baby's nap. It took some real schedule scrambling to pull it off but I managed to not let my writing change the family life-style.

Eventually I wrote more, started teaching at conferences and presenting my workshops on time stewardship. Trips away from home were limited to once or twice a month.

This past year our medical bills got out of hand and I started working part time at the local school. With those five mornings I lost my cherished flexibility, gained a whole new perspective on juggling my time and found a new respect for my working sisters.

I am grateful that I had those precious early years home with the children. I am also grateful for the way the Lord has brought me through in cycles so I haven't tried (or had to try) doing it all at once.

CHRISTIAN WORKING WOMEN HAVE PRESSURES

There are specific pressures on the working women of today. Author Barbara Greenleaf observes, "Americans are experiencing an emotional time lag between the supposed ideal, mothers who devote their entire day to child nurture and the real, mothers who need and want to work."[7]

Our mothers and grandmothers also received more support and affirmation from their families and society than we do. While statistics show the two-career couple as the majority, they are treated like an unpopular minority. Often this is especially true in the Christian community.

The pressures on the Christian working women of today come from various sources—

From Our Husbands

Greenleaf notes that working mothers are considered neither a status symbol nor a source of pride in many circles.[8] Many husbands feel that a working wife reflects their own inadequacies.

As Carole said, "I know my husband hates my having to work. I keep telling him it's not his fault . . . just part of the economic picture, but he still sees it as his personal failure."

From Our Churches

In many Christian circles there is a sense of righteous criticism against women working outside the home. "If you would just cut out the extras—."

"We've always had enough faith in God to provide for our needs without me going to work."

"Are you some sort of libber?"

Much of the criticism from the Christian community is a direct backlash from the women's liberation movement. But as one tired young working mother said, "I'm not working for liberation's sake but for survival."

From Our Health

The wife and mother who receives satisfaction and fulfillment from her job will still have numerous stresses and time pressures. But the woman who is stuck in a job out of financial necessity has multiplied stresses and new health threats.

The incident of stress-related heart disease is 7.9 percent for women in general. For men it jumps up to 15.3 percent. For the working woman who does double duty as "full-time" wife and mother the figure leaps to 21.3 percent. The high risk group is composed largely of women who do clerical work, care for children and have blue collar husbands. They work for economic reasons at jobs where they have little authority.[9]

From Our Time

When we start working outside the home our total workload increases as we try to balance our many roles and responsibilities. Statistics show that women who work outside the home have 10 hours less free time per week than men or full-time homemakers.

The full-time homemaker spends approximately 40 hours a week on housework. The employed woman a little more than half that. But that's on top of outside job hours. Today's women are still responsible for the home no matter how heavy their work load.

In spite of conveniences from food processors and word processors "women today put in three hours more a week on household chores than their grandmother did fifty years ago."[10]

As a result of all these we are under more time pressure than any generation before. We battle words like "stress" and "burnout" that were not even part of our mother's vocabulary.

"What really separates the working mother from the rest of the world is time. You probably have less of it in which to do more things for more people than do most of the other men, women, and children on this earth."[11]

Much of our identity as a woman is wrapped up in how we take care of our home and family and how we think other people see us. As one woman wailed, "There are days when I don't feel I'm doing any one thing well, because there are just so-o-o many demands for my time."

In a close-up report in *Ladies Home Journal* they asked women aged 25-55 what the hardest thing is about working.

They all answered, "finding enough time."[12]

Transition

The picture of the American woman of today looks like a city under siege. Yet bleak as the picture appears it is also full of excitement for Christian women. It is a picture full of new opportunities, of new growth, of transition. And transition is always tough.

But as Christian women, this transitional time can ultimately be used for our good and God's glory if we appropriate the wisdom and empowering that God has already provided for us.

Interwoven with our walk with the Lord are all the resources we need for stress control, mental health and the wise stewardship of our time.

"I have called you by name; you are mine. When you go through deep waters and great trouble, I will be with you. When you go through rivers of difficulty, you will not drown! When you walk through the fire of oppression, you will not be burned up—the flames will not consume you. For I am the Lord your God, your Savior" (Isa. 43:1-3, *TLB*).

Chapter 2
Management or Stewardship?

"Let a man regard us in this manner, as servants of Christ, and stewards of the mysteries of God. In this case, moreover, it is required of stewards that one be found trustworthy" (1 Cor. 4:1-2, *NASB*).

I have often read about time *management*, but have trouble with the term management. I define management as meaning control and with that definition comes built-in frustration. It has always been my experience that while there are many things I can do with time, control definitely is not one of them.

As Rev. Ben Patterson says, "There is a frantically preposterous dimension to the very idea of time *management*. Who do we think we are anyway, attempting to subdue time?"[1]

In 1977 our pastor started a series of sermons on stewardship—stewardship of money, talents, prayer and *time.*

The concept of stewardship of time was new to me and I grew increasingly fascinated as I took notes:

- All our time belongs to God.
- We will be held accountable as to how we use our time.
- God should be glorified by how we use our time.
- We either use time, waste it or redeem it.
- We are to redeem our time (redeem meaning to buy it up while it lasts).
- We need a balance in our Christian living. Not all praying, not all playing.
- Time is for investing, not just spending.[2]

I was intrigued with the concept of stewardship and many of my old questions regarding the usage of time were answered during Pastor Wes Jeske's sermons.

What Is a Steward?

A steward is a person entrusted with the management of the affairs of others. The steward doesn't own the possessions, but is designated by the owner to manage them.

> What do we mean by being "stewards of our time"? Is it really our time we're talking about, or is it God's time? Has it been granted to us, along with the gift of life itself, to be disposed according to our own purposes . . . with only a portion of our own determining going back to Him from whence it came? Or as Charles Shedd suggests, since God fashioned the world and all that is in it, does *all* our time belong to Him?[3]

In Matthew 25:14-30 Jesus tells about the master who entrusted his money to his three servants. One buried his share for safe keeping. The other two doubled the master's money and when they returned his money, it was, of course, more than they were entrusted with in the beginning. That is good stewardship.

To each of those two servants the master said, "Well done, good and faithful servant! You have been faithful with a few things; I will put you in charge of many things."

As with our money, we are to be fruitful with the time the Lord has given us.

In *Decision,* Victor Adrian describes the characteristics of a steward:

1. Accountability: a steward is not free to do what he wants; he is directly and ultimately accountable to God for the way in which he has fulfilled his responsibility before God.
2. Dependability: a steward will be judged according to his faithfulness in fulfilling the purposes God intended for him.
3. Availability: a steward is always a person under orders.[4]

Spending or Investing?

We were playing a game the other evening and I laughed as 10-year-old Benji complained about how fast the sand in the little hourglass ran through. "It just isn't fair!" he sulked.

Just like adults, I thought. We are each entrusted with the same amount of time, yet we so often complain, "My time goes so-o-o fast!" "She has more time than I do!"

As I watched the hourglass, I mused about my life. *Is it pouring out like so many grains of sand? Am I spending or investing?*

Time stewardship is our focus: not just cramming more into our already too busy lives or spending more money but learning to be stewards, learning from the Master steward, learning to invest.

Part Two
Time Stewardship: New Testament Models

Mary of Bethany was sitting in her favorite spot at Jesus' feet. It went against all custom for her to be there, but the men who were with Jesus had grown familiar with her quiet presence.

I have learned so many things from this man, mused Mary. *His actions are always in step with His words. I've learned as much from watching Him as from listening—*

He is teaching these men He calls disciples to pray and He often draws apart from us all to talk with His Father. He always looks so refreshed when He comes back from these times.

This Jesus has a unique sense of time. He never is in a frantic rush like my sister, nor does He dillydally like I often do. He frequently makes mention of time, like He is moving in tune with a schedule from His Father.

He is the Messiah, yet not only does He command us to love one another, He shows us how. When He walks down the

dusty roads, all manner of poor, sick and lame people crowd around Him.

He always takes time to speak, to touch, to heal. Just the other day a group of little children were swarming around Him like bees to honey. He held them and laughed with them and told them stories.

"And she had a sister named Mary, who seated herself at the Lord's feet and was listening to His teaching" (Luke 20:39, *Amp.*).

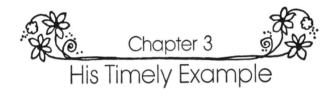

Chapter 3
His Timely Example

"He said, 'It is finished,' and bowed his head and dismissed his spirit" (John 19:30, *TLB*).

Christ had most of the emotions and experiences that you and I have in an average day: love for His mother (John 19:25-27), anger (Matt. 21:12), sorrow (John 11:35) and fatigue (Mark 4:38). Yet I have never found a record of His yelling at little children, "Get thee away from me, I'm busy!" Nor is there a record of Him complaining to God, "But how can I possibly accomplish my task in three short years? I just don't have enough time!"

How did He accomplish so much, with such lasting results, in such a short time? How did He gain the peace of mind to know that He had done all that He was supposed to do, even though He left behind multitudes of unhealed, untaught and unsaved people?

The example Jesus sets for us in the New Testament provides the foundation for the rest of this book. The most exciting
part of my research on time has been seeing not only Jesus'
example, but discovering its relevancy to my life today.

Prayer

Jesus prayed early in the morning and late at night. There
are numerous accounts of His going "out into the mountains to
pray" (Luke 6:12, *TLB*), of being "alone, praying, with his disciples nearby" (Luke 9:18, *TLB*) and His telling them "to sit
down and wait while he went on ahead to pray" (Matt. 26:36,
TLB).

Too often we pray, then rush to work out our own answer.
Jesus not only prayed often, but He waited for both His
Father's orders and the strength to carry them out.

If Jesus, the very Son of God, recognized His need for time
with His Father, how much more should we?

Priorities

I have often felt the need to right every wrong, adopt every
needy child, take in every stray cat and write every good book
and article. But then I realize that even Christ left some things
undone. No one (but me) expects me to do it all.

In Luke 4, Satan tempts Christ to bypass the program of
redemption He had designed with His Father in ages past.
Satan wants Him to use His power to feed Himself by turning
stones into bread. If He consents to worship the devil He can
have the kingdom of the world without going to the cross. If He
leaps off the Temple roof He can convince the Jews that He is
Messiah without dying and rising from the dead.

Satan's suggestion that Jesus be and do more than God the
Father had intended is the root of the temptation. But the Lord
Jesus knew that it was part of His Father's eternal priority that
He go to the cross, and nothing could deter Him.

> Jesus did not finish all the urgent tasks in Pales-
> tine or all the things He would have liked to do, but
> He did finish the work God gave Him to do. The

only alternative to frustration is to be sure that we are doing what God wants.

Nothing substitutes for knowing that this day, this hour, in this place we are doing the will of the Father. Then and only then can we think of all the unfinished tasks with equanimity and leave them with God.[1]

Planning

God had specific plans for Christ's earthly ministry and in Luke 14:28-31 Jesus advocates good planning when He asks, "Who would start constructing a building without planning and counting the cost?" and "What king would go to war without planning with His counselor?"

Christ's life is a perfect example of a planned life, from childhood, "I must be about my Father's business," to the end of His life, "It is finished."

Proprietorship

"I knew I was accountable for the things I did, but I never realized that God owned my time," a young wife and mother told me after a workshop.

Jesus knew He had only three brief years for His earthly ministry. God was the proprietor of His time and He made that time count.

> Jesus' time was filled, but He did not let Himself be controlled by people or circumstances. Rather He consciously chose how He would invest His time in dependence on the Father. He knew what His work was and His only purpose was to complete His task.[2]

And He knew whom His time ultimately belonged to.

Punctuation

Jesus was surrounded by crowds wherever He went. They followed Him, begged for healing and touched His garments.

He didn't turn them away—He healed the lame and fed the crowds.

Even little children swarmed to Him, yet He never saw them as unwelcome interruptions to His day. He paused to hold the children and issued strict warnings to those who wanted to send them away.

Jesus also knew that His times of teaching, preaching and healing needed to be punctuated by breaks of restful leisure. He did all that was essential to His Father's plan, but kept a sense of balance.

At times Jesus went away from the crowds with His friends and disciples. He visited at the home of good friends. He stopped in the midst of a storm to take a nap.

There are records of Jesus attending weddings, banquets, going fishing and having picnics—times for restoration and enjoyment.

People

In Jesus' example of the balanced life He always made time for investing in people. The investment of friendship is exemplified in the recordings of His frequent contacts with Mary, Martha and Lazarus. Yet even in His leisure time with friends Jesus had an awareness of the need to prepare His friends and followers for the time when He would be gone. Thus He lovingly chided the busy Martha and encouraged Mary to sit and listen to Him.

One of the basic rules of good time stewardship with people is training others and delegating responsibility. Jesus constantly employed those principles as He invested in the lives of His disciples.

He taught them to pray. He taught them about the heavenly Father both by word and action. He made them a part of His ministry and showed them how to spread the gospel. He prepared them for the time when they would be physically sep·arated from Him and ministering on their own.

Even here with my children, in a drafty old Victorian house, those lessons on investing are as alive and relevant as they were when Jesus sat on a boat and shared them with a band of scruffy fishermen. They are a direct parallel to our roles as Christian parents.

We teach our children to pray. We teach our children about their heavenly Father by word and action. We make them a part of our everyday ministry and teach them to spread the gospel. We prepare them for when they will be separated from us and ministering on their own.

Perfection

How often have I heard, "When I have the perfect office I'll write too," "When I have the perfect study time I'll teach a Sunday School class," and "When I find a perfect church I'll join."

Jesus didn't wait for perfect people or perfect conditions to carry out His plan. "He spent huge amounts of time with so-called second-class citizens: tax collectors, prostitutes, lepers, disabled, Samaritans."[3]

He took a bunch of scruffy men and used them in different roles—Paul, who had been the biggest persecutor of Christians; Peter, who tried to walk on water and floundered; and Thomas, with his doubts and questions. Jesus used these very human, very imperfect people to record His life and spread the gospel. Neither did He wait for a perfect temple to preach in. He taught crowds from a ship, fed crowds from a few loaves and fishes and turned water into wine. Because He knew He was in His Father's *perfect* will He didn't waste time waiting for perfect people or situations.

Pace

> Jesus our example never appeared rushed. No record is made of Him being in a frantic hurry. For every person He taught thousands didn't hear His teaching. Yet He didn't hurry. His life had balance and a sense of timing. He didn't ruin His gifts with haste.[4]

Not only does God have a special pace for each of us, but

that pace will differ from person to person. Too often we ruin those gifts with our haste.

Pressure

The people at church think I should teach a Sunday School class, my mother hints that I should call every week like my brother, my husband tells me of a friend who irons all of her husband's clothes, "including his underwear," the kids urge, "but Jimmy's mother *always* lets him," and my editor calls to ask when I'll be finished—the pressure is on.

We think of stress and pressure as a modern phenomenon, but 2,000 years ago in dusty villages Jesus also knew stress and pressure:

- From His mother: "Child, it's time to leave the Temple and come home with us" (see Luke 2:48).
- From Satan: "If you're really the Son of God jump off this Temple roof" (see Luke 4:11).
- From the people: "The crowds searched everywhere and when they finally found Him they begged Him not to leave" (see Luke 4:42).
- The religious leaders complained about His eating companions (see Luke 5:30) and tested Him with trick questions (see Luke 10:25).
- His friend and frequent hostess, Martha, not only applied pressure for Him to chastise her sister but chastised Him herself when Lazarus died (see John 11:21).
- On the night before His crucifixion the disciples couldn't stay awake with Him (see Luke 22:46), Peter denied Him (see Luke 22:54-62) and He was framed by an angry mob and mocked.
- Even as He hung, dying on the cross, the thieves being crucified on either side pressured Him. One taunted Him with insults while the other beseeched Jesus to remember him in Heaven (see Luke 23:40-43).

Three years of constant stress and pressure. How did He handle it all? In *Spotlight on Stress,* Dr. Gary Collins writes,

First, He knew His priorities—why He was here

and what He wanted to accomplish. Second, He had His values straight. He sought to do the work God had given Him . . . He spent time *every day* meditating alone with His Father.[5]

Jesus had all the powers of the universe at His command. Yet when He had to cope with stress and pressure, He used two *simple* resources that are available to each and every one of us 2,000 years later—time alone with God and an intimate knowledge of the Scripture. The Head Steward sets the perfect example for us as we pursue our study of time stewardship.[6]

My Pacesetter

The Lord is my pacesetter,
    I shall not rush.
He makes me to stop
    for quiet intervals.

He provides me with images of stillness
    which restore my serenity.
He leads me in ways of efficiency
    through calmness of mind,
        and His guidance
            is peace.

Even though I have a great many things
    to accomplish each day,
I will not fret
    for His presence is here.

His timelessness, His all-importance
    will keep me in balance.
He prepares refreshment in the midst
    of my activity by anointing my mind
        with His oil of tranquility.

My cup of joyous energy overflows.
    Surely harmony and effectiveness
        shall be the fruit of my hours,

And I shall walk in the pace
    of the Lord
And dwell in His house
    forever.

—Author Unknown

Chapter 4
Mary and Martha of Bethany

"As Jesus and his disciples were on their way, he came to a village where a woman named Martha opened her home to him. She had a sister called Mary, who sat at the Lord's feet listening to what he said" (Luke 10:38-39, *NIV*).

"You're a Mary, aren't you?" I asked my quiet friend. Ethel spends hours involved with in-depth Bible study, leads Bible study groups and writes Bible study books.

"Very definitely!" Ethel answered. "Marthas always wear me out."

"Well," I replied, "if Mary had helped out a little Martha could have listened too."

"But," my Mary friend asked softly (Marys always ask softly), "would she have sat still long enough to listen?"

We both started laughing, "We'll never know, will we?"

Balance

Mary and Martha have always held a certain fascination for me. They are the two halves of the whole I want to be.

The Martha-me finds so much that needs to be done that the Mary-me is constantly having to assert herself to protect the truly necessary.

The Mary-me could easily study and worship to the exclusion of more practical things. Together the Martha-me and the Mary-me blend for a well-balanced whole.

I like the way Fay Angus puts it, "We have Mary saying, 'Don't count on me. I'm listening to the Word of God,' and we have Martha holding the bag and saying, 'Good grief!' The answer is in balance, priorities and timing . . . . "[1]

Models

Mary and Martha walked in sandled feet along the dusty roads surrounding Bethany (actually Mary walked, Martha bustled). Some 2,000 years later we modern-day Marthas and Marys find the dusty Bethany roads replaced with the fast lane. Yet we are still faced with the same basic choices faced by our Bethany counterparts: serving or worshiping? doing or being?

God's biblical economy is amazing. No words are ever wasted and each biblical anecdote usually has both an obvious message and a deeper one. So it is with the story of Mary and Martha. The obvious is a historical account of two sisters who knew and loved Jesus. The deeper message is applicable to our lives today.

These sisters from ancient Bethany offer lessons for our contemporary Christian lives; lessons both positive and negative. Taken separately Mary's and Martha's weaknesses are all too obvious. But when their qualities of service-worship and doing-being are combined, they model the balanced woman I aspire to be.

Hospitality

Our first introduction to Mary and Martha tells us, "as Jesus and the disciples continued on their way to Jerusalem they came to a village where a woman named Martha welcomed them into her home" (Luke 10:38, *TLB*).

The village of Bethany was near Jerusalem and after that first visit the home of Martha seems to have become a favorite stopping place for Jesus on His way to and from the city. During the three years of Jesus' public ministry He was homeless and the open hospitality must have been especially precious to Him.

Attributes of a good hostess are doing the necessary things to make the honored guests comfortable (Martha) and making that guest feel important by attentive listening (Mary).

Planning

Since all the references call it "Martha's house" we can conclude that she was a widow. And as all "household executives" know, it takes much planning to keep a house running smoothly.

Martha's household included her brother and sister, and she held "open house" for Jesus who undoubtably was accompanied by some of the disciples.

Mary also did some planning of her own. In John 12:3 *(TLB)* we are told of a dinner held in Jesus' honor where Martha served (planned and organized). "Then Mary took a jar of costly perfume made from essence of nard, and anointed Jesus' feet . . . . " Mary must have planned in advance for this act of adoration (just as we all need to have some planned worship in our lives) to have had the costly perfume with her.

Priorities

In our lives we are constantly weighing and reassessing priorities. Mary and Martha are models for us by having Jesus Christ be their number one priority.

When Jesus is allowed His rightful place in our lives, He will come ahead of *everything else.* Mary and Martha exemplify this in different ways.

When Mary sat at Jesus' feet she "ignored the custom of her day which would bar her, a woman, from sitting to talk with male guests. Her love was too strong for such restrictions."[2] Mary was harassed by her sister, and probably others, for defying those conventions. Yet she still was compelled to absorb all she could of Jesus' teaching.

Martha showed bravery in sharing her home so freely with Jesus. During the last months of His earthly ministry He was often in danger. To openly associate with Jesus of Nazareth at that time (especially so close to Jerusalem) presented the possibility of danger to Martha.

But custom and danger were of no importance to Mary and Martha when compared to the precious time spent with Jesus. This should be true with us.

Stress

When Mary and Martha were faced with stress they reacted within the framework of their personalities and temperaments. When she thought Mary wasn't doing her share of the work Martha snapped, "Sir, doesn't it seem unfair to you that my sister just sits here while I do all the work? Tell her to come and help me" (Luke 10:40, *TLB*).

Then Lazarus died and the mourning sisters received word that Jesus was coming. Martha went to meet Him, but Mary stayed home weeping.

In both cases—Martha's fretting and Mary's mourning— they had taken their eyes off Jesus and were seeing only the situation. The results of taking our eyes off Jesus are still devastating.

Be Yourself

Choleric Martha wanted Jesus to make quiet melancholy Mary get up and serve like she was doing. We each have different needs, goals and priorities and so we must each approach our use of time with our uniqueness in mind.

Instead of Marthas and Marys trying to force each other into a cookie cutter copy of themselves we need to affirm each other—the Marys and Marthas alike.

Worship

When we think of worship Mary usually comes to mind. But Martha worshiped in her way—with her hands. She personifies love-in-action because Martha's service was an act of worship.

In *I Came to Love You Late,* Joyce Landorf writes,

> When He was in her home, Martha found herself unable to do enough for Him; His presence in her house inspired her to unbelievable heights of giving and doing. She could not put her finger on the exact reason for her desire to serve Him, only that it was so. It was as if He had touched a responsive chord deep within her being and serving Him became her most compelling urge.[3]

Mary spent much time at Jesus' feet: sitting and listening (Luke 10:39), in supplication when Lazarus died (John 11:32) and in total adoration when she anointed Him with oil (John 12:3).

Between the two sisters there is again illustrated the need in our lives for balance. The wisdom and strength we need for our times of work and service are empowered by our necessary times of adoration and worship.

Occupied

Martha in the kitchen, serving with her hands,
  Occupied *for* Jesus with her pots and pans,
Loving Him—yet fevered,
  Burdened to the brim,
Careful, troubled Martha,
  Occupied *for* Him.

Mary on the footstool, eyes upon the Lord,
  Occupied *with* Jesus, drinking in His Word.
This the one thing needful,
  All else strangely dim,
Loving, resting Mary
  Occupied *with* Him.

So may we like Mary choose the better part,
  Resting in His presence, hands and feet and heart,
Strengthened with His grace,
  Waiting for the summons,
Eyes upon His face.

When it comes, we're ready,
  Spirit, will and nerve—
Mary's heart to worship,
  Martha's hands to serve.
This the rightful order, as our lamps we trim:
  Occupied *with* Jesus—
Then occupied *for* Him.

                              —Lois Reynolds Carpenter

Part Three
Time Stewardship: Personal Inventory

Martha had slipped on a loose rock by the baking oven and twisted her ankle. Gentle, melancholy Mary was determined to take her sister's place in running the household that day.

Just for today I'll try to be like Martha, Mary vowed to herself. She skipped her morning quiet time on the flat rooftop and went straight to the kitchen.

By lunch time Mary had broken Martha's favorite clay crock and burned the bread that was to have been Lazarus's breakfast.

Mary ran a trembling hand through her long dark hair. *I make a horrible Martha,* she cried out in frustration.

Martha was resting on her pallet with her swollen ankle propped up on a pile of goatskin pillows. She couldn't remember the last time she had been in bed during the daylight hours.

Ah-h-h, she murmured, *a whole day to be like Mary. I'll gaze out the doorway at the blossoming trees. Mary's always talking about their beauty, but there's never time to look.*

Martha looked out the door at the blossoming trees. Instead of enjoying their beauty she realized how soon it was until harvest and thought of all the extra work she would have to do.

Oh-h-h, Martha sighed, *I make a horrible Mary.*

"Now Jesus loved Martha and her sister and Lazarus; [they were His dear friends and He held them in loving esteem]" (John 11:5, *Amp.*).

Chapter 5
Personal Inventory

"Study to shew thyself approved unto God, a workman that needeth not to be ashamed, rightly dividing the word of truth" (2 Tim. 2:15, *KJV*).

The purpose of time stewardship is not to turn out cookie cutter clones of superwomen. In fact, one of Martha's mistakes was in trying to mold Mary into another busy, activity-oriented Martha. We are all one of God's unique creations and each of us function differently. By studying ourselves and celebrating our individuality we can learn to go with the current rather than constantly fighting against it.

"Defining who we are is literally an exercise in building personal stability. Explicit personal definitions equip us to turn our detours into scenic side trips leading to maturity."[1]

The more we can learn about ourselves and how we best

function the more wisely we will be able to use our time. One of the major keys to stress control, preventing burnout and having positive mental health is in knowing ourselves. Stress pioneer Hans Selye emphasizes the importance of knowing ourselves and often advises, "Decide if you're a race horse or a turtle. Then structure your life accordingly."

During the months prior to my fortieth birthday I started to get better acquainted with myself. I used the worksheets that are a part of this chapter and I restudied books on spiritual gifts and temperaments. In the process I have made many new discoveries about myself. Some I like and some I'm trying to change. Almost everything I have learned about myself will ultimately affect how I use my time. I urge you not to skip over the next few pages. Get acquainted with yourself before proceeding.

In the book *Praying with Power,* Lloyd John Ogilvie writes,

> We are so much more than the outward person others see. He wants to liberate the unique, distinctly different person each of us is . . .
>
> Sin is to miss the mark of the reason for which each of us was born. It is also the refusal to be the unique miracle each of us is. Christ sets us free from whatever binds the special person inside us.[2]

In my time of introspective study I discovered that I have a melancholy temperament, am an introvert, more accomplishment oriented than people oriented. I am not a saver, I am present-future oriented and not nostalgic.

I am also a Martha with a strong devotional life. I am a morning person. I am visually oriented and I function best in clean, uncluttered spaces.

Can you see how each of these characteristics will have an effect on my time stewardship?

Gordon Lindsay writes,

> Just as the earth itself has a purpose, so God has a

purpose for every soul created in His image and placed in this world. God has a blueprint for every life. It is sad that 99% of the human race never realize the calling for which they were created![3]

Some suggestions before you start: find some quiet time, a comfortable chair and a sharp pencil. You may answer these pages at separate times or all in one session. Try not to censor your answers (no one else needs to see them) and be careful to answer as you really are—not as you want to be. Don't feel hampered by the space limitations on these pages—feel free to use ruled paper, a "me book" or your journal.
Now it's get-acquainted time—

Who Am I?

How many different descriptions can you think of?

Labels and roles: wife, mother, homemaker, career woman, etc.

Who am I? wife

Who am I? mother

Who am I? Pastor's wife

Who am I? Homemaker

Who am I? B. Study leader

Who am I? Clerical officer
Counselor

Characteristics: quiet, athletic, good listener, etc.

Who am I? Quiet
Idealistic

Who am I? Sluggish o lazy
Selful,

Who am I? Good listener
Artistic

Who am I? Discerning
Conscientious
Self critical Procastinator

"A good name is more desirable than great riches . . .
(Prov. 22:1, *NIV*).

Getting Acquainted with Me

1. Am I a Mary or a Martha? Neither
2. What are my spiritual gifts? (See 1 Cor. 12.) Discernment
3. What is my personality type? Reserved love
4. Am I a morning person or a night person? Morning
5. Am I a high-energy person? No Definetely No
6. Do I have to ration my strength? Yes
7. What are three of my favorite activities? Reading Needlework Ironing
8. When was the last time I did any of them? Today
9. Am I visually or auditorily oriented? Visually
10. What is my ideal work environment? Tidy but homely
11. Am I an introvert or an extrovert? Introvert
12. Do I have a large circle of friends or a select few? Select few
13. Am I over/under involved with outside activities? Under
14. How do I handle stress? Reasonably badly
15. How do I prevent stress? Needlework
16. What are three things I do best? Needlework, Bstudyleader
17. What areas of my life most need improvement? Housework social life
18. What three things are most important to me? Husband, child & God
19. What three people have influenced me the most? Mother husband friend
20. Am I people oriented or achievement oriented? people
21. What circumstances need to change for my happiness? House to be clean & tidy
22. How do I deal with life's little problems? Push aside
23. What three words would I use to describe myself? Lazy weak Selfish
24. What part does God play in my life? Large part

"But grow in the grace and knowledge of our Lord and Savior Jesus Christ" (2 Pet. 3:18, *NIV*).

What Do I Believe?

What is my personal theology? Am I coasting along, going to church (why?), calling myself a Christian (why?) more out of habit than knowledge or insight?

If being a Christian was a crime would there be enough evidence to convict me? Can I present enough positive evidence?

After you answer, open your Bible and check it.

My personal definition of God: One who is in control of my life

My personal definition of Jesus Christ:

My Saviour

My personal definition of the Holy Spirit:

My helper & teacher

My personal definition of the Trinity:

One God

My personal definition of salvation:

Trusting in Jesus' death on the cross

My personal definitions of heaven and hell:

Somewhere wonderful & peaceful
Somewhere awful and painful

My personal definition of the Bible:

Basic ruler to measure our lives by.

My personal definition of prayer: Communicating
with God

My personal "life verse":

Rest in the Lord

My personal testimony:

I believe that Jesus took the punishment
that was due to me when He died.

My personal reasons for being a Christian:

There is no peace in any other
religion or ideology like the peace of
God through salvation

My personal reasons for attending church:

To worship & praise God and to
learn from His word as taught in
the pulpit.

"We believe and know that you are the Holy One of
God" (John 6:69, *NIV*).

In Five Years I Will Be—

"Before you can do something you must first be something."

—Goethe

Spiritually I will be:

Physically I will be:

Emotionally I will be:

I will be doing:

"We should make our plans—counting on God to direct us" (Prov. 16:9, *TLB*)

Time Inventory

1. When is my best free two-hour period? *Sunday pm.*
2. What is there about me physically that helps or hinders my use of time? *Sluggishness & laziness*
3. What is there about my current life cycle (small children? aged parents?) that affects my use of time? *Work outside the Home.*
4. Am I naturally organized? *No*
5. Do I have a realistic sense of time? *No*
6. How am I hurting myself by the way I use my time? *Dissatisfied*
7. How am I hurting others by the way I use my time? *Lack of time*
8. How am I hurting God by the way I use my time? *Lack of time*
9. Am I satisfied with the amount and quality of time I spend: in daily devotions? with my husband? with my children? with myself? *No* *yes* *yes* — *Could be better*
10. What is my biggest time challenge? *Housework*
11. What area of time usage do I most need to improve? *Home time*
12. Do I regularly evaluate my priorities? *Yes*
13. What part does goal setting play in my life? *Very little. Never attain*
14. Do I use a schedule? *Sometimes*
15. Do I have trouble saying no? *No*
16. Am I over committed? *Yes*
17. Do I have any time management tools?
18. What are my worst time-wasting habits? *TV soaps*
19. What are my community involvements? *Nil*
20. What are my church involvements? *B Studies*
21. What is the most frustrating part of my time usage? *Not enough*
22. Is relaxation, fun and exercise a part of my day? *Sometimes*
23. How does my use of time reflect my relationship with God? *I don't know.*

"My times are in your hands . . . "   (Ps. 31:15a, *TLB*).

Role Models

School children play this game often. They emulate stars, sports figures, their teachers. But as adults, we are taught not to envy, not to copy. There is a place in our lives for positive peer modeling. If you discover that you especially admire Sue's gift for hospitality or way with decorating, ask her to teach you. She will be so flattered she can't refuse.

My ideal woman would have:

the Bible knowledge of   *Carol*

the friendliness of   *Pat*

the creativity of   *Anne McArthur*

the musical abilities of

   Anne McA.

the organizational skills of

   Catherine Fraser (Kyle)

the homemaking skills of

   Catherine (Kyle)

the mothering skills of

Anne McA.

the wifely attributes of

Pat MacAskill

the hospitality of

Jean Madood (Falkirk)

the looks of

Christine Gardiner

the style of

Christine Gardiner

the personality of

Pat McAskill

"A kindhearted woman gains respect" (Prov. 11:16, *NIV*).

These Are a Few of My Favorite Things

Sprinkle these in your daily schedule like fine seasoning.

1. Looking out the window
2. Looking through a Kaleidoscope
3. Reading
4. Painting
5. Needlework
6. Listening to music
7.
8.
9.
10.
11.
12.
13.
14.
15.
16.
17.
18.
19.
20.

"Whatever is true, whatever is noble, whatever is right, whatever is pure, whatever is lovely, whatever is admirable—if anything is excellent or praiseworthy—think about such things"

(Phil. 4:8, *NIV*).

What Do I Do?

A friend once compared herself and what she accomplished with others. She was constantly putting herself down because she didn't "measure up." After keeping a time journal and recording each activity she was pleasantly surprised at how much she actually accomplished. Her self-esteem received a healthy boost. Writing out exactly what she did helped her see the difference between her concept of time usage and its actuality.

List everything you accomplish during an average week:

"In everything you do, put God first, and he will direct you and crown your efforts with success" (Prov. 3:6, *TLB*).

Why Am I Doing This?

"If you're spending less than ⅔ of your time doing things you want to do, you're not performing up to your potential."

Dr. Charles Garfield
Family Circle

Activities I am doing and want to do:

Activities I am doing and don't want to do:

Activities I want to do but am not:

"Each one should test his own actions" (Gal. 6:4, *NIV*).

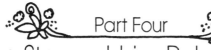 Part Four

Time Stewardship: Relationship Priorities

Mary was sitting near Jesus. She knew there were other things Martha thought she should be doing now: embroidering a new girdle, that tunic mending for Lazarus, and preparing the meal.

Martha is always so busy doing things for people, Mary thought. *I just like to be with them.*

Mary recognized her need for quiet, for times of refreshment and infilling at the feet of Jesus. After these times she was better able to love the people around her.

She often frolicked with the servant's children and sat and talked with Lazarus. And with her gentle humor Mary even had a knack for coaxing infrequent laughter from Martha.

"There is really only one thing worth being concerned about. Mary has discovered it—and I won't take it away from her!" (Luke 10:42, *TLB*).

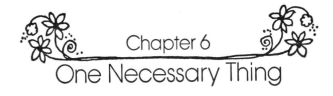

Chapter 6
One Necessary Thing

"Evening, and morning, and at noon, will I pray, and cry aloud: and he shall hear my voice" (Ps. 55:17, *KJV*).

Quality relationships should be the foundational basis of our lives: relationships with Christ, our families, friends and the Body of believers.

We live in a materialistic society that too often uses people and treasures things. A world that measures success by things: degrees achieved, money earned, awards won. But biblical priorities still put people and relationships first and God still cares more about who we are than what we accomplish or collect.

Not only is investing in relationships biblical, but its importance is also recognized by psychologists:

Over and over again students are demonstrating

that quality relationships are the only universal factors that will definitely alleviate the damaging effects
of stress.[1]

In today's pressure-prone society there are additional benefits:

Sorting out priorities can be a good pressure
releaser. When you face the facts that no job no
matter how important supercedes your relationships to God and your family, much of your tension
and stress may be resolved. Some things that
seemed vitally important to you before may shift
their positions to lower levels of value.[2]

A television host once asked me, "What do you see as
options for the first three priorities of a woman's life?" I unhesi-
tantly replied, "As a wife and mother I don't believe we even
have an option. Our first three priorities must be God first, our
husbands, then our children. After those three the options
start."

My answer was based on the order of creation. God created
the heavens and earth, dark and light, dry land and water,
growing things and animals. Then He said, "Let us make man
in our image."

The first relationship created was between Adam and God.
Of all the possible relationships that would eventually be established the first was with God, "the only relationship that defines
our worth."[3] The order of relationship priorities was established.

Examples

Jesus invested His life and His love in people. The New Testament is full of His relationships, from the disciples to the three
siblings in Bethany. Even while dying on the cross, Jesus was
making arrangements for His mother's care.

The relationships in Jesus' life are recorded in loving terms.
John is called the disciple whom Jesus *loved;* Luke is the

beloved physician; and we are told that Jesus *loved* Mary, Martha and Lazarus.

As beautiful as these relationships were, the outstanding relationship Jesus modeled was the one He had with God the Father. Even if He had to leave people untouched and untaught His first priority was that time with God.

In *Quiet Time,* the author asks, "If He who was never out of touch with His Father could not dispense with definite and prolonged seasons of retirement for fellowship with Him, how much less can we?"[4]

The primary source of Jesus' strength and power on earth is still available as our primary source of power and strength—consistent, daily time with God.

"Now the report of his power spread even faster and vast crowds came to hear him preach and to be healed of their diseases. But he often withdrew to the wilderness for prayer" (Luke 5:15, *TLB*).

The Word and Our Walk

Experts say that our walk with God is the most significant factor in how well we manage our time.[5]

One psychological study done on a group of Christians showed that the maturity level was consistently and proportionately related to the time spent with the Word. Those who spent time daily with the Word were found to be more mature, more mentally healthy and to show no significant pathology.[6]

We cannot go further in service *for* Christ until we have gone deeper in fellowship *with* Christ.
—Daily Bread

In spite of biblical admonitions, examples and studies like the above, the average Christian spends 60 seconds a day in prayer.

The Need

Rev. Wesley Jeske says, "When we feel the least like praying we need to most. When we have the least amount of time we need prayer the most. There are times when it's easy to pray and times when we need to discipline ourselves to pray."

Respondents agreed with the need for more consistent devotional time:

Marjorie: "I'm fighting Satan in this department. I find my daily devotions the most difficult thing of all to allow for."

Michelle: "God is as much a part of my schedule as I let Him be. I have to ask Him to take over parts of my life, but then I'm always collecting them and forgetting to give them back to Him. I often hold on to the worthless causing the loss of the priceless."

Karen: "I'm totally dissatisfied with the amount of time I spend on daily devotions. It's the one area I feel I lack the most control over. Funny—I like my quiet time with God. It's just that I can't seem to maintain it as a priority."

Kaye: "It seems to be a low priority unless I'm going through a really rough time. Too often it gets left until the end of the day when I'm tired and would rather sleep than read or pray."

Set the Tone

We all function differently and I have friends who have terrific devotional lives that include prayer and study in the afternoon or late evening. My husband often has his devotions after the kids and I are in bed—I have my devotions in the morning. I tease that between the two of us we have the day covered. But whatever our preferred time for devotions and Bible study if we can start the day with at least a brief time of prayer and Bible reading we set the tone for the rest of the day.

Martin Luther often said, "Today I am going to be so busy that I must spend the first three hours in prayer." Most of us can't spend three hours each morning, but we need to realize the importance of making prayer a priority in all our days, not just trying to "fit" God into panicked situations and already packed schedules.

Linda gets up 45 minutes before the rest of her family. She combs her hair, washes her face, and has 30 minutes of quiet time with the Lord before starting her day.

Anne wakes up late, hurries through the house waking her family. There's no time for breakfast and she feels "strangely" out of touch with God all day.

That first half hour sets the tone for the rest of Anne's and Linda's day. Like Linda, I learned years ago that I can't rely on my puny supply of adequacy and strength. Life for me is only possible by appropriating—through prayer—God's power to flow through me.

Hours?

How much devotional time is ideal? How much is enough? Elaine answers, "How much is enough? I always want more!"

Linda adds, "I spend an increasing amount of quality time each year, but it never seems enough."

Our devotional times change with the cycles of our lives. Joy writes, "Finding enough devotional time is always a struggle, but it's much easier during this empty nest time."

When our children were preschoolers I got up at 5:30 A.M., because it was about the only uninterrupted time I could find. When I was home full time and all the children were finally in school I took an hour after they left in the morning. Now that I leave for school with them I have 30 minutes for prayer and Bible reading between the time my husband leaves for work and the children get up.

Once a year I try to set aside a whole day with the Lord. I pray, sing from a favorite hymnal, read a Christian study book and start praying again. I've found this to be a special way to help heal "the never have enough" feeling.

In *Praying with Power,* Lloyd John Ogilvie writes,

"As we think in our hearts, so are we" (see Prov.

23:7). We become what we think about all the time and if the Lord is given access to our thoughts in only a brief time of prayer each day, we will become less than the persons He intends us to be .... Wings of prayer lift us above the present pressures so we can get perspective and receive power to be maximum for the Lord.[7]

Or Minutes?

I cherish the longer periods of time with the Lord, but like most busy mothers I have discovered numerous ways to "keep in touch" during almost any available moment.

Every morning while I get dressed I listen to a 30 minute radio Bible study (I read over the study guide at some other time). I usually read a few chapters of a good Christian book before I go to sleep.

My interpretation of "pray without ceasing" (1 Thess. 5:17) is to have running prayers throughout the day. When I arrive at school I pray for the children and for God's love to shine through me. While I'm ironing I pray for whoever's clothes I'm pressing. While I'm cooking I pray for our mealtime together.

We live in a rural area with long open spaces between our county and the rest of the world. I get in hours of prayer during my driving time.

Linda humorously adds, "I have a running conversation with God throughout the day. Without it I'd probably weigh 482 lbs., lie around watching TV and pity myself to death."

Susanna Wesley realized the need for frequent prayer and knew how to get it. When her numerous children saw Momma with her voluminous apron over her head they knew she was praying and was not to be disturbed.

Daily Plans

Most of us shudder at the thought of starting off on a trip without studying a map. We study the map *before* we start—not after we are lost. Yet we often wait until the last minute to seek God's direction through prayer. When I remember to present my day's schedule to the Lord for His blessing and refining, it is amazing how much smoother the day goes. By taking our plans to God first we can avoid many of our last-minute cries for help.

Benefits

The purpose of my personal time stewardship, the workshops and this book is to have my time under God's management so I can have a constantly growing relationship with Him.

Although that is my main purpose, there are numerous other benefits. Proverbs 10:27 tells us, "Reverence for God adds hours to each day." Daily devotional time (reverence) will not actually add more hours, but with God's help and discernment it will certainly seem like more.

Jenny: "The more time I spend with God the more time I seem to have. To learn to be a good steward of time I need to spend time with the chief steward."

Regina: "My relationship with God is the total answer to my usage of time. As long as my priorities are right, as long as I am depending on Him and walking with Him and recognizing that He is in full control of my life—I have enough time."

Elaine: "When God is given His rightful place in my life and day, then there seems to be time for everything else He sends my way."

Pat: "When He's first, other things seem to fit into place and I can see things from His point of view. When my focus is right, I'm more able to accept the unexpected and cope with everyday pressures. The Lord keeps my focus clear and gets me back on track."

Suggestions

"I'm constantly being fed," the intense woman told me. "I have my Christian radio station on all day long." I love Christian broadcasting, but there is a subtle danger in allowing the electronic media to replace our private, personal time with the Lord. No matter how eloquently the radio or television pastors pray, their prayers are not to be substitutes for our own.

If you don't have a regularly established time for prayer and Bible reading, here are a few simple suggestions for getting started. But a word of warning: this is addictive and the more time you have with the Lord the more you'll want!

1. Set a minimum of 15 minutes each morning.
2. Use a brief devotional booklet like *The Daily Bread,* published by Radio Bible Class, Grand Rapids, MI, or *The Upper Room,* published by The Upper Room, Nashville, TN.
3. Divide your time between prayer and Bible reading.
4. Keep a notebook to record what you're learning and answers to prayer.
5. Use biblical resources and good books on prayer.
6. Get involved in a Bible study.

Interwoven

Picture a circle. Our relationship with God is the basis for our being able to be good stewards of our time and good stewardship is how we protect that vital relationship.

Not only is time stewardship and our walk with God interrelated, but the other relationships of our lives can only be as strong and healthy as our relationship with God.

Devotional Checklist

1. How many times per week do I have devotions?

2. How long do I usually spend?

3. Does this seem like enough time?

4. Do I have a good balance between prayer and Bible reading?

5. When is my best uninterrupted time?

When you're faced with a busy day save precious time by skipping your devotions. —Satan

Got a Minute, Lord?

Well, Lord, there are some days
    when I feel like 40,000 people
    have tramped through my life—
"Where is this? Can I have that?
Excuse me, are you busy?
Can you help me?"

Most of the time I don't mind.
But I can understand why you never wrote a poem
    or a song or painted a picture.
Did you miss the quiet carpenter's shop
    with its clean smell of shavings,
    Joseph's beloved plane,
    each tool worn to fit your fingertips?
Did you miss that feeling of accomplishment
    from making simple benches or tables?
Yet you never said, "Go away" to anybody.

Was it because you could see beyond
    their small questions,
    to their real needs—and you loved them?
You loved them so much you didn't want them
    to leave unsatisfied.

Help me to see the needs beneath the masks.
Help me to trust you for the right time
    for everything,
    to not be upset when other people need me,
    and to remember that
What I want done now may not be necessary
    at all.

—Janet Machalowski
Reprinted with permission from an article which appeared in the March, 1978
issue of *Christian Herald Magazine.*

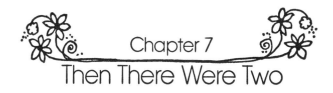

Chapter 7
Then There Were Two

"The Lord God said, 'It is not good for the man to be alone. I will make a helper suitable for him'" (Gen. 2:18, *NIV*).

"Help!" A hand shoots up during one of my seminars and a woman asks, "There's never enough time for just us. What can I do?"

It is ironic that the second area women express as a major time problem is also the second highest priority—quality time with husbands. Our relationships with our husbands should rank in importance just after our relationship with God.

After the creation and the establishment of earth's first relationship—between Adam and God—God realized something was missing. Then God created Eve.

God created Adam and Eve as friends, husband and wife, lovers and co-workers at least nine months before they were parents. The Bible says, "a helper for him," before it mentions Eve as a mother. Even before there were in-laws priorities were set: "For this cause a man shall leave his father and his mother, and shall cleave to his wife" (Gen. 2:24, *NASB*). Again the biblical priority was established. First and foremost is our relationship with God, then with our husbands.

Marriages most often in trouble are those where God-ordained priorities have been changed.

Investing

In one chapter we can't possibly do an in-depth study on marriage. However, we can discover various ways to invest time in our husbands.

When our children were younger and I was dealing with their numerous time and energy-consuming physical problems, it was a constant challenge to invest time in my marriage relationship. But I realized then that the seasons would eventually change and the children would leave home. The time spent on our marriage 20 years ago was not only enjoyable but was an investment in our future.

One evening when our children were younger a neighbor came over as I was feeding the kids and commented on the fact that Dennis and I weren't eating with them. I explained that we would be having a quiet dinner-for-two after the children were put to bed.

"That's just too much trouble for me now," she replied. "We'll wait until our children are grown for things like *that*."

"I'd be afraid," I softly answered.

"Afraid of what?" she queried.

"Afraid that if we wait that long, we won't have anything to talk about."

Those intimate dinners are even more challenging now. Not only can all the children stay awake later than we can, they delight in teasing the "old folks" for acting mushy. But those dinners are still worth the time and effort.

First Place

There are numerous ways to say I love you. Ways to let our mates know they occupy first place. My husband, Dennis, has a chronic physical problem that requires frequent and lengthy tests. I make a point of driving him to the hospital lab. I read or edit while I wait for him. When he reappears, I put away my work and drive him home.

He's a "big boy" now and he can drive himself home. I don't have to go along, but it's a small way of saying, "I care about you and you're important to me."

Every year my husband's company sponsors an all-day conference. They have workshops and lectures. Dennis invites me, but never insists that I accompany him.

As much as I love my husband and try to keep up-to-date on his work, I have to admit that spending a whole day hearing about auto parts is really pushing my interest span.

Last year Dennis suggested I come along and bring my briefcase. We had breakfast out, an hour's drive alone, and while he was in meetings I sat on an anonymous hotel sofa and worked. He came and got me for lunch and I worked the rest of the afternoon. We had dinner together after the conference and a leisurely drive home. He was impressed that I invested a whole day in him and his work and I probably accomplished more than if I had stayed home.

Even in the busiest of schedules we can find innovative ways to invest in our marriages. Susan has started getting up early to fix her husband's breakfast. A small thing, but again it sends out a powerful message.

Accentuate the Positive

James Kilgore writes, "A husband will do almost anything to live up to the compliments and pride of his wife."[1] I am firmly convinced that one of the biggest time wasters of American wives is putting down their husbands. Studies have shown that for every negative thought we must come up with at least 5-7 positives to undo the damage. Don't waste time on put-downs. Instead we can make a daily list of positives about our mates, concentrating on positives that they can live up to.

Love Notes

Most of our husbands spend 8-12 hours a day away from us at work. When I realized this I tried to come up with ways to encourage and affirm Dennis during those long hours (also to remind him of me!).

I have put notes in Dennis' sandwiches—"Life without you would be like a ham and cheese sandwich without the cheese" (the note replaced the cheese). I have also put Scripture verses in his lunch bag and written "I love you" with a black marker on a banana.

Last Valentine's Day I sent a big balloon bouquet to Dennis at work. Periodically I send him wacky greeting cards (his co-workers have all decided we're nuts) and when I'm away I hide notes all over those areas of the house Dennis frequents.

Next time you are out shopping pick up a couple of cards for your husband—or a big yellow banana and a marking pen.

Communicate

One of the best time investments we can make is learning to communicate (not just report or complain) with our husbands. I've heard a marriage counselor say that of all the troubled marriages he has counseled none communicated even 15 minutes a day.

Dennis and I both tend to hold things in and the area of communication is one at which we have always had to work. We have used several different Bible studies on marriage and communication and found them invaluable.

Plan

Some of our most meaningful times together are spontaneous. As Gloria says, "More and more I'm resisting the felt obligation of staying home with the children or maintaining the home to do something spontaneous with my husband."

But we can't depend on the unplanned to keep our marriages well and healthy. We need to have some planned time for each other.

Pat: "There is never enough time together to satisfy either of us. We are now attending an adult Bible study together and it's been great."

Carla: "No matter how tired we are we spend time together at the end of every day."

Darlene: "Because of his long work hours we *must* have some planned time together and that time is a high priority."

Joint Activities

When Dennis and I were first active in the church we stopped one night to take stock of what was happening. While we were both involved in church work and various aspects of ministry, we were never together. His meetings were always on different nights than my meetings. On Sundays I sat with the choir. When we had communion, Dennis served and we couldn't sit together then either.

Many churches have now realized this problem and are rescheduling meetings and services with families and marriages in mind.

Spending time together is a good way for bonding to occur within a relationship. Dianne's husband travels a lot and she often makes arrangements for the children and goes with him. Regina is involved with all the outdoor sports that her husband is interested in. Darlene's husband just leased a new office complex and they worked together to decorate.

One of the common strengths of a healthy marriage is time spent together. How much time have you spent together this week?

In an article in *Family Life Today,* Norm Wright asks:

- Do I seek out activities or duties that prevent me from being with my spouse?
- Do I tend to give my spouse leftover time?
- Do I use the TV, newspapers and so on as excuses to avoid dealing with my feelings about our relationship?
- Does my use of free time help or get in the way of my marriage relationship?[2]

Dates

Dates. Dating. In a house full of teenagers those words are used frequently. There's excitement, suspense and romance.

Unfortunately after we get married the dating aspect ends.

"We can't afford a baby-sitter, we can't afford a dinner out." We've gone through numerous times of not being able to leave the house because of children recovering from surgery and tight money situations due to a large family. But there are ways around these problems.

Trade off baby-sitting with a friend. Feed the children and set the table with candles after they go to bed. Have hot dogs by candlelight if you can't afford to go out for steak.

I have surprised Dennis at work by arriving to take him out to lunch, gotten up early so we could go out for breakfast, and even kidnapped him for a weekend.

We have recently started walking together. After dinner the children clear the table and Dennis and I go for a walk. We hold hands, talk or walk in silence—we are together.

The divorce rate is skyrocketing and is almost as high for Christians. One of the leading causes is time pressure. You won't often see it that way for it is usually disguised as "money problems," "work pressures" or "sex problems." But a careful look at the root problem is the lack of quality time.

So often we are busy earning a living and/or raising a family that the marriage relationship becomes a casualty, another sad statistic.

We need to periodically look at our marriages and ask again: Am I spending time or investing?

Then There Were Two Worksheet

1. How much time per week do I spend with my husband?

2. How much of that time is spent communicating?

3. When was the last time I told my husband that I love him?

4. When was the last time we prayed together?

5. How often do we have an evening just for us?

6. How long has it been since we shared a fun activity?

Chapter 8
Then There Were Three

"Children are a gift from God; they are his reward" (Ps. 127:3, *TLB*).

Oswald Chambers has said, "Spiritual truth is learned by atmosphere, not by intellectual reason." We need to provide that atmosphere for our children.

"An inefficient home is a pressure prone place, while a well-ordered domain creates an atmosphere of peace and well-being."[1]

What am I teaching my children about time stewardship? Is what I'm teaching consistent with what they are seeing in the atmosphere of our home?

In our large family we have a variety of temperaments and time users. The one who is the most disorganized, who is always losing school books, reports, homework, library books, one shoe, and five coats last winter most often puts himself in a pressure situation. I have learned much from him about how we cause our own pressure. What is he learning from me?

Who's First?

When a group of new fathers get together they often compare notes on who has the most perfect child. However, they will eventually complain about the changes in their homes and marriages since the arrival of the baby.

Babies are helpless and totally dependent little beings and it is no wonder it is such a struggle for us as mothers to keep our perspective straight. A plaque I saw sums it up, "We owe our children love and a home. We don't owe them first place." That position goes to our husbands.

With our priorities established, we move on to spending (investing) time with our children. The debate rages about quality time versus quantity time. The ideal is, of course, to have large quantities of quality time. When the size of our family seemed to explode in a short time period I talked to mothers of large families on how they managed to find time for each of their children. Many of the ideas that I have personally used and that are in this chapter I gleaned from these experienced ladies.

Finding Time

When we first realized the need for more individual time with our children I anticipated spending hours with each child. I soon discovered that time seldom comes in large chunks. But I have been pleasantly surprised by the brief moments together that fit into different times of the day and areas of the home.

Mornings

For a time our eldest daughter ate an early breakfast with Dennis and me. She needed time away from the younger children. Many mornings she would share problems and concerns with us that she wouldn't have at any other time.

When Tim and Robby were on the late schedule at school we sometimes used the time between chores for devotions or a quick game. One winter Timmy and I set up a Ping-Pong table, complete with score pad, near the washer and dryer. We would play a few minutes each morning while I did the laundry.

Kitchen

"Someone help me with this frosting" is an effective lure for help and after licking the bowl the indulger gets to wash it. There are numerous kitchen activities for every age, but these should be separate from regularly assigned chores.

All of our children had favorite foods when they were younger: Julie was the macaroni and cheese expert, Robby loved making jam, Becky liked the "add water and bake" mixes. Benji specialized in toast. Unfortunately, Tim has always thought of the kitchen as a short order cafe.

Now that the children are older we have a new plan where they alternate planning, fixing and cleaning up dinner one night a week.

Dinner Time

Each night at dinner it is someone's turn to say the blessing. Benji knew "Robby-day" and "Timmy-day" long before he knew the regular names for Tuesday and Wednesday.

The dinner table provides other opportunities for special times. The secret is picking nights at random, not just holidays and birthdays. A canceled meeting is reason enough for a party. Consequently the neighbor children have at times thought we were slightly daffy:

"Can you play?" one would ask.
"No, we are having a party," Robby would answer.
"Oh, whose birthday?"
"Nobody."
"Oh, then why the party?" the bewildered child would ask.
"Well," Robby would answer, "it's Monday."

The star would have his/her choice of dinner. We would each say something special about the honoree and for grace we would each give a brief "thank you" prayer.

Family Devotions

We have tried almost every possible form of family devotion. The keys seem to be flexibility and frequent evaluation. We started with one night a week set aside for devotions and fun.

For a couple of years we got together with another family for a combined family time. Dinner, games and crafts were enjoyed together and then we would split by ages for devotions.

We have family conferences where we try to deal constructively with faults, complaints and problems. As the children grow older we find that with a house full of teenagers it's almost grab 'em when you can.

Sandy has devotions each morning with her boys that include a prayer for the day, a featured Scripture verse and a devotional reading. Darlene and Kathy reported that they use Sunday afternoon for special family times.

Summer Vacation Outings

During summer vacation I take one child grocery shopping with me each week. They get some extra attention; I get some extra help.

I also take each child out for a day. We shop for school or camp, have lunch, wander through the toy store. It's understood that the key word is Mommy's time and not her money.

Schoolwork

Schoolwork provides opportunities to be alone with the children. I can listen to the younger ones read even when cooking or mending.

When Tim was having speech therapy, I had to work with him 20 minutes a day. My first reaction was negative because there were five other kids at home then. However, it turned into a very precious time and when he was released, we shared the victory.

Love Me Best

I once heard a story about a family with an uncommonly

wise mother. After she died, the adult siblings reminisced. "I was always Mother's favorite," recalled the first.

"I thought I was," said the second. They soon discovered that she had given each child the unspoken impression that he was her favorite.

By wisely investing time in our children they can each feel, "Mom always loved me best."[2]

To My Grown-up Sons

My hands were busy through the day
I didn't have much time to play
The little games you asked me to
I didn't have much time for you.

I'd wash your clothes, I'd sew and cook
But when you'd bring your picture book
And ask me please to share your fun
I'd say, "A little later, son."

I'd tuck you in all safe at night
And hear your prayers, turn out the light
Then tiptoe softly to the door
I wish I'd stayed a minute more.

For life is short, the years rush past
A little boy grows up so fast
No longer is he at your side
His precious secrets to confide.

The picture book is put away
There are no more games to play
No goodnight kiss, no prayers to hear—
That all belongs to yesteryear.

My hands once busy now lie still
The days are long and hard to fill
I wish I might go back and do
The little things you asked me to.

—Anonymous

Then There Were Three Worksheet

1. How much quality time a week do I spend with each child?

2. Do my children feel I am available for them?

3. Do I have a regular "program" for passing on my values and beliefs?

4. When was the last time we did something fun together?

5. What are my children learning about time usage from me?

Part Five

Time Stewardship: The Psychology

The Teacher was coming! Martha was happiest when she was serving Him. She pictured His smile and the feelings of peace and love that emanated from Him.

But—

There was so much work to do. Extra food had to be prepared and rooms readied. Martha rolled up her sleeves and wrapped a piece of rough cloth around her clean tunic.

As she mixed the ingredients for bread, Martha tried to shake off the pounding in her head and the tightening of her neck muscles.

"But Martha (overoccupied and too busy) was distracted about much serving; and she came up to Him and said, Lord, is it nothing to You that my sister has left me to serve alone? Tell her then to help me—to lend a hand and do her part along with me.

"But the Lord replied to her by saying, Martha, Martha, you are anxious and troubled about many things"
(Luke 10:40-41, *Amp.*).

Chapter 9
Stress

"You will experience God's peace, which is far more wonderful than the human mind can understand. His peace will keep your thoughts and your hearts quiet and at rest as you trust in Christ Jesus" (Phil. 4:7, *TLB*).

The honored guest has arrived, thought Martha, *and there are dozens of last-minute details to see to. The dates need to be stuffed and no one has set out the goat cheese. So many things to do and where is Mary?*

Martha is a classic example of stress. Her problem was not her desire to serve Jesus. She got into trouble when her priorities got out of kilter and she attempted to do more than was necessary.

Stress. Tension headaches. Ulcers. Heart disease. Depression. Breakdown and burnout. Stress was Martha's nemesis in long-ago Bethany and is not only considered a phenomenon of our fast lane era, but has also been labeled the number one health problem in the world.

Defined

When asked to define stress most people mention death, divorce, getting fired. All are negatives. All are catastrophic. But stress isn't always caused by catastrophic negatives, nor is all stress harmful.

"Our bodies can't tell the difference between going to the dentist or falling in love, between being promoted or losing your job. When stress occurs, the stress response is never far behind."[1]

Stress pioneer Hans Selye defined stress as "The body's nonspecific response to *any* demand on it, whether that demand is pleasant or not."[2] Dr. Dennis Hensley succinctly defines stress and offers a solution: "Stress is a sickness for which time management is the medicine."[3]

Women Under Stress

Twice as many women as men suffer from depression. In an article in *Psychology for Living,* author Robert H. Weber cites several reasons and theories for this:

- social roles: women often see themselves as accountable for everything;
- body chemistry: due to hormonal fluctuations;
- feelings: women are often feeling oriented and dwell more on *how they feel* rather than *what they do;*
- images: trying to live up to the Superwoman image.[4]

Today's Marys and Marthas have more varied demands than ever before. While our grandmothers worked hard, they were generally under less stress because their boundaries were clear and their roles defined.

We have more options today than at any other time in history. But often the options and choices are without definition. Times of transition are times of stress.

Our second adoptive child had always been in a world defined by the bars of playpens and cribs. Shortly after Benji joined us we went to visit a friend in the mountains. I put 15-month-old Benji down in a big grassy field.

Freedom and unlimited choices spread out as far as he could see. Benji looked left, right, front and behind. Then he burst into loud wailing, overwhelmed by the choices.

Good Stress—Bad Stress

Stress is a mixed blessing. Without the proper amount of stress (positive tension), all the drapes in our house would droop, sag or fall. Without the proper tension neither my sewing machine or my daughter's violin would function properly.

But when there is too much stress (negative tension) the rod breaks, the thread snaps, there is no music. So it is with people. Without some pressure we wouldn't accomplish anything. There comes a point with me where I have a deadline or company is coming, and I am supermotivated, spurred to action. I shift into high gear. I feel invigorated and challenged.

Past a certain stress point and I snap like the sewing machine thread. I feel overwhelmed, swamped by the multiplicity of the demands I perceive. At this point I am ready to retreat to a corner and hide from the world.

WHAT ARE THE CAUSES OF STRESS?

A Counselor Speaks

Barbara Winchester is a counselor at Gardenview Christian Counseling Services in Hayward, California. When I asked Barbara about the correlation between time stewardship and stress control she said,

> In my years of counseling I have discovered that those persons who are inept at disciplining their time are unstable in many ways. They are often either overly active or withdrawn and under involved. The more disorganized they are and the longer the condition continues the more scrambled their thoughts and emotions.

Overload and Perception

Martha had prepared many meals before. She had entertained many people before. The difference during one of Jesus'
visits was overload: she took on too much—or so Martha felt.

The everyday stress of my life-style might do someone else
in, but I am used to the emergencies, noise and innumerable
doctor appointments that come with parenting a large family
with many special needs. It is only when my tolerance level gets
overloaded that I start getting into stress trouble.

I thought about our perceptions of stress when I read, "We
each see the world through 'stress-colored glasses' and what is
unbearable for me might be a piece of cake for you."[5]

I have a friend who has three grown daughters and weekly
household help. A stressor for her is not having the maid show
up. She views my life in a big, awkwardly laid out house, with
assorted pets and children running through it, with something
akin to horror.

I have another friend who has a house larger than ours
filled with twice as many children as we have. I view her ultra-
busy life-style with horror.

The problem for my two friends and me is not so much the
stress but our perception of stress.

> Some of us who've never had the earth move
> under our feet have still experienced the physical
> effects of stress. I concluded that it's not what hap-
> pens to me in life but how I process what happens
> to me that determines whether or not I'm a likely
> candidate for the ill effects of stress."[6]

Cycles

As women, our ability to cope with stress can be cyclic.
There are usually more daily stressors during the cycle of preschoolers than during our fifties. We can deal with these life
cycles by accepting them as such and not trying to crowd
everything into today.

Monthly cycles also affect our coping abilities. When I first started having trouble with premenstrual tension it almost knocked my socks off with its intensity. I saw my doctor who made some recommendations regarding diet and vitamins. I also tried to plan my schedule so that heavy-duty things weren't on deck for those times when I knew I wouldn't be coping well with stress.

Unpredictability

Gary Collins tells that those things which are predictable are less stressful. This can be a special problem for those with young children when it often seems that everything is unpredictable.

Schedules and plans help in this area. By anticipating as much as possible we can eliminate much that could be unpredictable stress.

Accumulation

In late 1979 we made a major move from a city of over 140,000 to a rural community of 1,700 people. The move was a desired one but did entail some drastic life-style changes. New schools, new jobs, new friends.

Within the first six months after our move the house flooded, Dennis developed a chronic health problem, our eldest daughter had an appendicitis attack and Becky was in a bus accident. Then one morning I woke up with a partially paralyzed face (Bell's Palsy) and the doctor gave me a prescription and told me to avoid stress. I have been a respecter of stress charts ever since.

I had not been prepared for the accumulated stress. After all, we had *wanted* to move. However, our bodies can't differentiate between positive and negative stress and the combination resulted in an overload.

Poor Copers

"Poor copers will crowd the time dimensions of a problem. Or they may take the opposite approach and extend the time factors beyond all useful limits."[7]

One afternoon I decided to replace all the shelf paper in the kitchen. It was the first time I had ever lived in one place longer than the life of the shelf paper. Consequently I had no concept of the time involved, but I had a plan: (1) empty cupboards, (2) take off paper, (3) put in new paper, (4) refill cupboards. My plan seemed simple enough.

I emptied the cupboards, wondering where all that stuff had come from. All available surfaces in the kitchen were soon covered.

Then I started pulling the shelf paper off. Well, actually, I tried to peel the shelf paper off. When I finally got all the old paper removed it was a simple job to measure and cut the new paper. However, when I went to put the new paper down I discovered it had assumed a mind of its own and was going to stick wherever it pleased—and it wasn't on the shelves.

When Dennis came home I looked like someone Erma Bombeck writes about. I was sitting in the middle of the floor with paper stuck all over me. I hadn't given a thought to dinner and the more frustrated I became the more tangled up I got.

My husband started laughing and unwisely asked, "Didn't you realize what you were getting into?" I burst into tears and *tried* to throw shelf paper at him.

I had crowded my time dimensions and created my own stressful situation. I had used a plan, but it was a plan without a time line.

COPING WITH STRESS

Time Usage

In a survey run by *Bostonia* on stress, the allocation of time was cited as a second major source of stress within marriage and the family (after money, before sex).[8]

Using the basic principles of time stewardship and helping our children apply them in their lives can help us manage this one major cause of stress.

Family counselor James R. Malone once told me, "Proper time management is a vital and essential part of developing good mental health. When we handle our time wisely we fulfill part of our purpose for existence: accomplishment and achievement.

> Well arranged time is the surest mark of a well arranged mind.
>
> —Pittman

Over and over in my research on stress I have found that the key to dealing with stress is our response. "Stress is neither good nor bad. It is a consequence of living in a dynamic changing world. It's an inevitable part of life. But how we choose to respond to that stress is all important."[9]

Lowered Expectations

In the *Work-Stress Connection* the authors write, " . . . you can either increase stress by speeding up to get more done, or lower your expectations about what you have to achieve and thereby lower your stress."[10]

This coping response was mentioned by many of those respondents that have entered the work force. When Darlene went back to teaching, her children were expected to do much more than when she was home full time. The house still looks clean and presentable, but Darlene knows about the little things that haven't been done. No one else even notices and Darlene handles the changes with her lowered expectations.

Planning

Poor planning can cause unnecessary crises. Because of the multiplicity of our children's special needs my life has a certain amount of built-in stress.

I've learned over the years to *try* to keep my life stripped of nonessential stresses so I can cope with the ones I know will pop up tomorrow. Whenever a new stress comes up (new child, another surgery), I reevaluate to see what can be temporarily eliminated during the time of heavy stress.

By controlling what factors I can there is more energy to cope with the unknowns. After reading *Living with Stress* I realized I was at least heading in the right direction. One trait of a person who handles stress and change well is "the capacity to convert uncertainty to manageable sized risks and tasks."[11]

Information

Dr. Gary Collins suggests, "It's difficult, but to some extent an individual can do self-innoculation—getting information before a coming crisis situation knowing what to expect and reassuring oneself."[12]

When Becky and I have faced our surgeries I have researched every possible aspect so that I was prepared to face them. By eliminating every possible stress, I could better handle all the built-in stresses of surgery.

Support System

When we adopted Becky and Benji we attended a parent support group for those of us adopting older children. When Becky was enrolled in a special school we attended a support group for parents whose children had physical handicaps. I mentioned the various specialized support groups to a friend. She listened intently then wailed, "Why isn't there a support group for plain ol' me?"

A basic stress control is having a support system of close friends and relatives to whom we can go with our deepest needs. Often just having someone to listen to our time stresses can help us see solutions and cope better.

The Physical

A break in routine acts as a potent stress release. Going for a brisk walk and other methods of exercise gives us new surges of energy so we can return to our work renewed.

If fatigue is a real problem for you, a trip to the doctor can help track down any physical causes. I recently went through months of dragging fatigue. A quick blood test showed I was anemic and a few months of iron restored my energy level.

Proper amounts of sleep help us cope better with stress. When I am going through a particular time of stress I try to make a point of getting extra sleep. I've learned how fast intense stress will deplete my energy reserves.

One busy pastor's wife routinely plans "robe days" for herself and her daughter. They sleep late, stay in robes and slippers all day and take frequent hot cocoa breaks.

Shortly after I started working part time, I was getting frustrated trying to get my writing research done and adjusting to a new schedule. I set one Saturday aside and declared I was spending the day in bed. It was so unusual that the children were shocked into leaving me alone. I got some rest, a break from my usually hectic Saturday routine and a lot of research done.

Relationship with God

It is so easy during times of stress to either give up out of apathy or blame God at the time we need Him most. Bill Bright says, "Frankly man is just not capable of coping successfully with the pressures of modern life without drawing on the supernatural resources of God."[13]

The times when we are best able to cope with the stresses of our lives are those times when we are walking most closely with God.

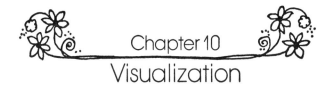

Chapter 10
Visualization

"For as he thinketh in his heart, so is he" (Prov. 23:7, *KJV*).

As a child I pictured in my mind the kind of life I wanted to live as an adult: it would be a big, old house with a loving husband, lots of children (at least one adopted) and we all loved the Lord. Part of the dream included books on a library shelf with my name on the covers.

My grandmother called it "daydreaming." My grandfather called it "woolgathering" and my teachers scolded me for wasting time. Today it's called positive imaging or visualization and is recommended by psychologists and theologians.

By whatever name you call it this is powerful stuff and can be part of some of my most productively spent time. Those images shaped my life and 30 years later are part of my present-day reality.

Power Tool

The first time I read about this powerful tool and exclaimed, "That's what I did!" was in Catherine Marshall's *Adventures in Prayer:*

> One of the most provocative facts I know is that every man made object, as well as most activity in your life and mine, starts with an idea or a picture in the mind.
>
> There is a connection between constructive dreaming and prayer. For in a sense all such dreaming is praying. It is certainly the Creator's will that the desires and talents that He Himself has planted in us be realized.[1]

Not only is visualization a powerful tool for shaping our lives but it can be used creatively to help us with our time usage. Rita Davenport writes,

> The day you wake up and stop thinking about what great potential you might have is the day you will probably fail forever. As long as you are satisfied with being unsatisfied in this life, you probably will be. Visualization is one of the most powerful tools I know that can aid you in planning for the successful use of your time.[2]

Last year I read *Seeds of Greatness* and it really had an impact on me. Denis Waitley writes that our minds cannot tell the difference between a real experience and one that is vividly and repeatedly imagined. "We perform and behave in life, not in accordance with reality, but in accordance with our perception and reality."[3]

> Picturize, Prayerize, Actualize
> —Norman Vincent Peale

Life Force

> [Studies show that imagination is a] life-governing device—that if your self-image can't possibly see yourself doing something or achieving something, you literally cannot do it. It's not what you are that holds you back, it's what you think you are not.[4]

What Denis Waitley writes about I have seen time and again in the workshops I present. There is always at least one woman who responds, "I'm hopeless. I'll never learn. I was born late and unorganized. I'm hopeless." With that attitude, I know there is little chance that she will be able to go home and manage her time any better than before.

Positive Images

How can we tap this powerful tool and use it to be better stewards of our time? Betty is going through a time of feeling swamped with her part-time job while caring for her big house and three children. Each night Betty flops into bed and mentally reviews her day—

I started off behind, the kids were all late for school and Joe was mad because I didn't get his shirt ironed. I was late for work again and in a crabby mood all day. I forgot to thaw the meat for dinner and everyone bickered until bedtime.

Betty goes to sleep thinking, *I can't do anything right and tomorrow will be more of the same.*

Tomorrow probably will be more of the same because she went to sleep with negative images reinforcing her behavior of the day.

Michelle stretches out in bed. She thanks the Lord for the good parts of her day, asks for forgiveness for some not-so-good parts and visualizes the next day.

Parts of her bedtime fantasy resemble the unreal perfection of "The Brady Bunch," but she does fall asleep with positive images dancing through her mind.

As Michelle falls asleep her last thoughts are of being in control and having a happy, successful day—reinforcing positive, future possibilities.

Whatever situation you find yourself in try to visualize in a positive light: an organized, efficient office, a successful dinner party, a home that is an oasis of calm in the midst of a hustle-bustle world.

Rehearsal

Whether it's for travel plans, speaking engagements or especially busy days, I picture myself successfully going through the process.

Each step of the way is walked through with Jesus, rehearsed in my mind and prayed over. I find the unknown often scares me and whether it's flying across the country during stormy weather or having major surgery, a successful visualization process takes some of the edge off that unknown quality.

If in the midst of my imagining a negative comes to mind, I rehearse how I will successfully deal with it. For a potential problem that I'm not sure how to cope with, I will stop and pray, "Lord, extra wisdom here," or, "help my energy level here," or, "more self-confidence here, Lord."

Susan adds appropriate Scripture verses with her short prayers.

In *Making Time, Making Money,* the author writes, "Real visualization isn't just daydreaming, it is picturing and imagining precisely how we wish to act or react to a future event."[5]

There are a few points that I have found in my adventures with visualization:

- Visualization is effective most any time, but especially so during rest time or before falling asleep.
- Picture each step of your busy day and walk through it, rehearsing each step.
- As you bump into anything negative, stop and pray for that particular possible problem.
- Keep the visualization positive.

After the dreaming comes the work and then the reality.

I learned at least this by my experiments. That if one advances confidently in the direction of his dreams and endeavors to live the life which he has imagined, he will meet with a success unexpected in common hours. He will put everything behind and will pass an invisible boundary.

—Henry David Thoreau

Visualization Worksheet

Goal:

Visualization:

Reality:

1. Write down one of your goals.
2. Continually visualize the successful completion of that goal.
3. Record the reality.

Chapter 11
Leisure Time

"Because so many people were coming and going that they did not even have a chance to eat, he said to them, 'Come with me by your-selves to a quiet place and get some rest'" (Mark 6:31, *NIV*).

Relaxation. Rest. Play. Leisure time. What is your initial reaction to these words? What images come to mind?

If your reaction to leisure is guilt and your mind's screen is devoid of images you're headed for trouble—but you have lots of company.

The word leisure comes from the Latin, *licere*, meaning "to be permitted" and one of our greatest needs is to be able to give ourselves permission to relax.

The respondents consistently put their own needs last (or not at all) on their priority lists. The need for leisure time is too often seen as an almost unattainable luxury and a source of guilt.

Surveys

In researching this subject, I found that other survey results matched the respondents' attitudes:

"Twenty-six percent frequently or very frequently had too little time to relax. Twenty-seven percent frequently or very frequently had too little time to pursue projects for personal enjoyment."[1]

In another poll not even one had an hour or even a half hour in the day to call her own.[2]

"Lack of leisure-time was a problem for over 50 percent of the women surveyed by the National Commission on Working Women."[3]

Respondents

Susie: "There just isn't any leisure time for me at this stage."

Kathy: "Leisure isn't a priority. I relax in the evening only because I've run out of energy."

Pat: "I find I become angry inside when there has been no time for me, since as wife and mother I have a lot to do with the tone of our home."

Karen: "No one better interrupt *M*A*S*H* or *Masterpiece Theater* and death to the person who wakes me up early on Saturday because these are my only areas of relaxation."

Darlene: "Once I accompanied another single friend playing tourist. We drove up the coast, walked on the beach, talked, prayed, rode in long silences. I started to unwind. But I don't do it too often. I feel too guilty."

Carol: "Leisure is one of the most necessary things for me but one of the first things to go when I start feeling pinched."

Joy: "I'm discovering more and more that fun times are necessary, but they have to be planned—it won't just happen."

Mary: "Fun time for me is through a theater ticket series, but I have to pay in advance so I'm committed and don't change my mind."

> If Christians do not come apart and rest awhile,
> they may just come apart.
>
> —Vance Havner
> *Daily Bread*

Women—Men

In one book women were surveyed on desirable leisure activity. They had trouble coming up with anything except sleep.

> In our culture the average man would not have this problem. He would be able to name sixteen things right off the bat that would make him feel good. That's because he's accustomed to having leisure time, to feeling that he deserves leisure time, and to indulging himself in that leisure time.[4]

The traditional picture is of the man coming home from work to a clean house and a well-prepared dinner. He stretches out in front of the TV and reads the newspaper.

Picture in contrast the woman returning from her day at work. She cooks that dinner and cleans that house.

This carries through to leisure activities. One young mother describes a typical episode: "Our family favorite is camping. New sights. New experiences. I love it! *But*—I still end up being responsible for night feedings, laundry and most of the meals."

Guilt

Many women report they recognize the need to relax and spend some time on themselves but always feel guilty when they do so.

Howard Hendricks has a colorful warning: "Relaxation is not wasted time and if you feel guilty it's because you've got an uneducated conscience and that thing will whip the living daylights out of you."[5]

Ruth Senter, author, mother and speaker writes,

Stress management includes knowing how to play. For those of us who are programmed toward work, play may bring guilt feelings. And who likes to feel guilty? Instead we drive ourselves with another project, another goal. Or we may go through the motions of play, but it is play with a purpose, not play for fun. Sometimes purposes get in the way of relaxation.[6]

Work Ethic

Why do we American women seem to have so many guilt feelings from our leisure time? Many of us are still victims of the Puritan work ethic. "Most middle-class Americans tend to worship their work, to work at their play and to play at their worship. As a result their meaning and values are distorted."[7] Chuck Swindoll warns,

We're programmed to think that fatigue is next to Godliness. That the more exhausted we are (or look!) the more committed we are to spiritual things and the more we earn God's smile of approval. The Christian's primary source of identity is fast becoming his or her work.

We would rather hear our family and other people tell us we shouldn't work so hard than face the possibility of someone thinking we lacked diligence. For many of us raised under the work ethic of our parents fatigue and burnout are proofs of the deepest level of commitment, to which I say—hogwash![8]

The phenomenon of burnout is partly due to the lack of rest and leisure in our lives. In the questionnaires many of the

7. Charles R. Swindoll. *Strengthening Your Grip,* copyright © 1982, p. 161; used by permission of WORD BOOKS, PUBLISHER, Waco, Texas 76796.

respondents reported that they had found extra hours to meet all their responsibilities—"I'm sleeping less."

The response of finding time by cutting out sleep and leisure is part of the trip to burnout. The first stage of burnout is overwork. According to Dr. J. Ingram Walker, a psychiatrist at Duke University and the author of *Everybody's Guide to Emotional Well Being,* the burnout victim is confronted by too many demands too often. Instead of coping properly she takes the step into the second stage herself. "Instead of taking a break," says Dr. Walker, "burnout victims eliminate exercise and recreational time in a desperate attempt to meet the demands placed on them."[9]

I'm reminded of the sage advice from A.W. Tozer, "Whenever you feel out of it spiritually, before you go into hours of morbid introspection, the first thing you should do is get yourself 12 hours of sleep."

Discipline

This entire chapter is of special interest to me because the lack of leisure has long been a part of my personal pattern. I was raised by my grandparents who instilled in me at a very early age the dangers of "idle hands." I learned my lessons well.

Having studied and learned the necessity for more balance, I must confess that there are times when the only way I can get myself to take a necessary break is by self talk: "If I take a break I'll be able to be more productive."

Ruth Senter has also had to work at her leisure time:

> I can never be a lay-back, soak-in-the-sun, smell-the-roses type of person. But I can be a productivity-achieve-your-goal type of person who has learned to loosen her grip on life and breath deeply of each moment. For some of us, relaxation is not a way of life. It is, instead, a learned response. Realizing that fact about myself was step number one in learning to manage stress in my life.[10]

Responsibility

We must also assume responsibility for our leisure. No one else will insist that we take it. When Darlene started teaching full time, she discovered that she *had* to schedule Saturday mornings away from home and kids. A few hours spent shopping, lunching with friends or getting spoiled at the beauty shop helped her go home and be a more relaxed wife and mother.

Guidelines

Leisure time is a rare treasure for most of us and I have had to follow a few guidelines to protect the leisure times I do have.

- Analyze what is relaxing to you and not what others think it should be. My husband, for example, delights in jigsaw puzzles. For him they are a relaxing diversion. Those strangely shaped pieces of cardboard drive me to distraction. My friend Jill relaxes by working in the yard. For me, that's forced labor. But give me a pitcher of iced tea and a good book—
- Stewardship also applies to leisure time. It is too easy to squander leisure time on a badly written book or a trashy TV show. Watching *Chariots of Fire* was well spent time; watching soap operas would be a waste.
- Leisure time in big chunks is wonderful, but I need to include small breaks in my day. "Joy breaks" I've heard them called: a long overdue phone call to a friend, a cup of tea, a walk.

> You will break the bow if you keep it always bent.

Chuck Swindoll points out that God created, communicated, then rested. "Omnipotence doesn't tire so God did not rest for that reason. He purposed to rest and sit back and enjoy His creation. Leisure again defined: taking time to imitate God."[11]

HOSPITALITY

I am sure that someone reading this book is wondering why I have included hospitality under leisure activities. Opening our homes to others *should* be a leisure activity but unfortunately we (like Martha) too often turn it into another source of stress.

One of the reasons why Martha was so uptight during Jesus' visit was that she had lost sight of the joy of serving Christ in her home and had focused on the many things she thought needed to be done.

Fellowship with other Christians should be one of the most basic aspects of our Christian walk. The three years of Jesus' public ministry were sprinkled liberally with times of fellowship—with the disciples, with crowds, with friends at Martha's house.

Unfortunately, one of the first things we tend to give up when things get rushed is sharing our home with others.

Those busy women who answered the questionnaires shared some simple, practical ideas for hospitality and this section is theirs:

Marjorie: "The most important thing I can think of is to pray for your guests before they come. It's even more important than cleaning your house. Prayer prepares their hearts as they come and quiets your spirit to receive them. Most people don't come to see your house—they come to see you. If the carpet is old, the furniture 'early garage sale,' and the rooms small— Christ's Spirit living in you will brighten and beautify your whole home."

Pam: "I attended a seminar and heard that entertainment is for our pleasure (to show off our cooking and home) while hospitality is for others (making them feel so welcome they don't notice the food and house)."

Merri: "I have four dinners that I make for company and I have the total menu on 3×5-inch cards. I also keep note of who's been invited, which menu was used and the date. I prepare the meal in advance and freeze it. I'm ready one hour before they come so I can relax."

Gloria: "Don't apologize for how the house looks. Let your welcoming smile be such that the guest will never see the dust."

"I make all our bread and most people consider this a treat."

"Be a good listener."

"Turn off the TV."

"Use simple menus so you're a relaxed hostess."

Diane: "Don't be fancy—just share yourself. I'll never forget a humble meal at a Sunday School teacher's home. I'll always be grateful for his willingness to share with us—his seventh grade class. It was a neat way to say 'I care about you and would like to know you better.'"

Karen: "I like to have friends over after church for coffee and sweets, to just talk or play games. It doesn't have to be fancy or a big deal."

Mary: "I like to concentrate on the guests and keep it simple—no gourmet meals or recipe expositions."

Darlene: "I used to think that as a single I should go to a couple's home. Now I invite not just singles but groups and families."

Linda: "We often invite families to the park for picnics and barbecues. It's a relaxed atmosphere, the food is simple and I don't have to worry about the house."

Jenny:

1. "Invite the Holy Spirit when you invite the guests.
2. I pray ahead that the love and peace of Christ will be evident.
3. I use easy-to-prepare food so I have more energy for my guests.
4. Do as much as possible ahead of time. People prefer your time and attention over exhausting schedules and elaborate meals.
5. Be a good listener. It's the most welcoming and hospitable thing you can do and will cover every shortcoming you have in other areas.
6. Really enjoy your guests and don't try to entertain them."

As newlyweds, Nancy and her husband wanted a special way to share their home with others and did so by finding out the anniversaries of couples in the church. We received an invitation and our choice of two dates. They met us at the door with a Scripture verse. A special theme meal had been prepared and we shared our favorite verse, song and how we met.

One of my favorite ideas for ingenuius hospitality comes from my friend Jean. For a time she lived in a small apartment and just couldn't fit all eight Wheelers in, but really wanted to minister to us. Periodically Jean would fix a meal, bring it to our house all prepared, then she and her husband would clean up after dinner.

The central message woven throughout all the responses on hospitality was that God isn't interested in a spotless house and gourmet food, but in our opening up our homes and giving of ourselves. Hospitality can also become a treasured time of leisure.

Hospitality

Sure, I believe in hospitality, Lord.
Just not *my* house.

We can't afford the fancy foods,
My dishes don't all match.
The living room sofa needs repairs
And what would I do with the kids?
You just don't understand, Lord.

But, my child, I do understand.

I never had a house, but I turned no one away;
When I fed the multitudes, it was with the plainest fare—
Borrowed fish and bread.
We had no dishes and no place to sit, but the ground.

It's you that don't understand, child.

Hospitality is not giving the fanciest food,
On your finest plates,
In an immaculate, childless home.
My kind of hospitality is a special kind:
Not things, not possessions, not treasures.

My kind of hospitality is sharing—
Yourself,

As I did.

                                    —Bonnie G. Wheeler

Leisure Worksheet

Your first assignment is to take time to read this poem written by an anonymous friar. After reading this lovely piece, write your own "If I had my life to live over again—"

If I had my life to live over again, I'd try
To make more mistakes next time.
I would relax, I would limber up, I would be sillier
Than I have been this trip.
I know of very few things I would take seriously.
I would take more trips. I would be crazier.
I would climb more mountains, swim more rivers, and
Watch more sunsets.
I would do more walking and looking.
I would eat more ice cream and less beans.
I would have more actual troubles, and fewer imaginary
ones.
You see, I'm one of those people who lives life
Prophylactically and sensibly hour after hour,
Day after day. Oh, I've had my moments, and if I
Had to do it over again I'd have more of them.

In fact, I'd try to have nothing else, just moments,
One after another, instead of living so many years
Ahead each day. I've been one of those people
Who never go anywhere without a thermometer,
A hot-water bottle, a gargle, a raincoat, an aspirin,
And a parachute.

If I had to do it over again I would go places, do
Things, and travel lighter than I have.
If I had my life to live over I would start barefooted
Earlier in the spring and stay that way later in the fall.
I would play hookey more.
I wouldn't make such good grades, except by accident.
I would ride on more merry-go-rounds.
I would pick more daisies.

Five things I enjoyed doing as a young child:
1.
2.
3.
4.
5.

Ten things I enjoyed doing as a teenager:
1.
2.
3.
4.
5.
6.
7.
8.
9.
10.

Fifteen things I would enjoy doing now:

Date of Accomplishment

1.
2.
3.
4.
5.
6.
7.
8.
9.
10.
11.
12.
13.
14.
15.

Hospitality Worksheet

My personal definition of hospitality:

Is hospitality a source of stress or pleasure? Explain:

How often do I usually have others in my home?

When was the last time I entertained in my home?

What is my most frequent excuse for not entertaining more?

Three Scripture verses on hospitality:

_____

I will invite:

I will serve:

Date:

Part Six
Time Stewardship: The Practicalities

Martha bustled around the house. It was time to start the preparations for winter. As usual, Martha had everything planned.

Lazarus would oversee the work in the fields and the storage sheds to see that they had grain for the long winter months.

Mary and some of the women would weave the cloth for the warm tunics and cloaks they would need.

Martha would work in the kitchen and by the end of the month there would be numerous containers of olives, wine and a variety of dried fruits.

Each night Martha was weary but content. Each item on her list was finished and right on schedule.

"So six days before the Passover Feast Jesus came to Bethany where Lazarus was, who had died and whom He had raised from the dead.

"So they made Him a supper, and Martha served" (John 12:1-2, *Amp.*).

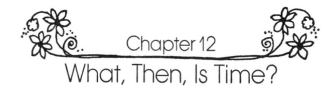

Chapter 12
What, Then, Is Time?

"The stork knows the time of her migration, as does the turtledove, and the crane, and the swallow. They all return at God's appointed time each year; but not my people!" (Jer. 8:7, *TLB*).

Time.

Seconds, minutes, hours, days, months and years—all stretching out before us in seemingly limitless array. We think we can borrow time, stretch time, ignore time and be healed by it. We frequently complain about our lack of time, yet we are all blessed with 1,440 minutes per day, 168 hours per week.

Webster's dictionary defines time as "indefinite, unlimited duration in which things are considered as happening in the past, present or future." Yet in spite of the lengthy definitions in my dictionary, I find myself in agreement with St. Augustine,

"What, then, is time? If no one asks me, I know; but if I want to explain it to a questioner, I do not know."

There is a ragged slip of paper in my files that gives ways in which the average amount of time is spent in a life span of 75 years:

> 23 years sleeping,
> 19 years working,
> 9 years in amusement,
> 7½ years dressing,
> 6 years traveling,
> 6 years eating,
> 1 year waiting,
> 6 months in worship,
> 19 days in prayer.

Whenever I read over that little list I think of my friend Lee Roddy who often tells classes of aspiring writers, "We do what we really want to do and make excuses for the rest." Keeping the above list in mind, that's a sobering thought.

Time is a river into which no man steps twice.
—Chinese saying

The people who followed Jim Jones to death in the jungle were the ultimate victims of abused time. Jim Jones kept his people constantly busy doing temple work. In his book on the Jonestown tragedy, *Deceived,* Mel White lists abuses that Jones practiced to keep the members of People's Temple in a constant state of deception.

> The members of the People's Temple worked day and night. Most of them spent their time doing good. Others of them spent their time doing evil. Regardless of the task each had, Jones made sure his followers were worn out. As a result they had no

time or energy to read, to contemplate, to interact with other people, to build personal or familial relationships, to gain perspective on the Temple deception or to do anything about it. They lived more and more in a zombielike state of obedience—too exhausted to care. And though at least temporarily exhilarated by their participation in Jones' utopian dream for them, in the end they were too exhausted to fight back when the dream became a nightmare.

Jones' victims were trapped by their own exhaustion. Are we tricked by guilt or pressure techniques (self-imposed or imposed on us by others) into doing jobs we don't want or really need to do? What other worthwhile tasks or opportunities are being sacrificed in the process?[1]

Can you picture yourself in a few years? Will you be like those poor people in Jonestown—nothing more than an exhausted zombie? Or will you be letting the Spirit of God direct how you are using your time?

In the previous chapters we have established our foundation: the biblical examples for time stewardship, our relationship priorities and the psychology. Now let's get into the nitty gritty of time stewardship. Some of this material might be old for you, other information might be totally new. Some skills you'll find you have been using for years and the rest might be uncharted territory.

Either way, tried or new, I pray that in the following chapters it will all come together for us so that we may continue to grow as stewards.

Time is the stuff of which life is made.
—Ben Franklin

Chapter 13
GOALS: Turning Dreams into Reality

"Forgetting what is behind and straining toward what is ahead, I press on toward the goal to win the prize for which God has called me heavenward in Christ Jesus" (Phil. 3:13-14, *NIV*).

The year 1969 seemed to mark not only the end of a decade, but also the end of hope. The media gave extensive coverage to hopelessness. The songs of the day lamented the death of hope and foretold of a world devoid of flowers, trees or breathable air.

In the early 1970s I was a volunteer at a drug abuse center. The young people I worked with believed all the media hype: they had no hope, no dreams, no goals. They lived only for the moment.

When we would ask, "But what about your future? How will the drugs you're taking now affect the baby you will want in

10 years?" their answers were always the same, "What kids? There won't even be a world in 10 years!"

They had no hope for a future; consequently they set no goals. One of the tragic results of that era were numerous babies born with multiple birth defects.

Goal setting is one of the abilities that sets humans apart from animals. My mellow gray cat has no plans, no goals and no ability to change. He merely drifts from nap to lap, feeding to feeding. But for us, life should not be determined just by surviving but by its distinctiveness and purpose.

> To be sure of hitting the target, shoot first and whatever you hit call it the target.
> —Ashleigh Brilliant

What Epitaph?

Can you smell the heady fragrance of flowers, hear the soft organ music, the muffled voices of the subdued crowd? Your funeral or mine? What will they say?

As we look down from our lofty clouds, will we be satisfied with the comments we overhear? As we stand before God and lay out all our earthly accomplishments, all the things we poured our time into, will they be received or burned as worthless hay and stubble?

What the mourners say and what is left behind will be a direct result of the goals and priorities we are setting now. We will not accomplish all the goals we set. We will change some, reevaluate some and totally blow others. But set them we must.

While failing to accomplish a goal doesn't make us a failure, the goals we set will define the people we become, the things we accomplish and the legacy we leave behind.

Elimination Game

At this point in my workshops I ask for a show of hands following these questions:

"How many of you have set a goal for this week?" A sprinkling of hands go up. (Always more after New Years.)

"How many of you have a goal for this month?" A few hands go down.

"For the year?" That usually eliminates the few remaining hands.

If there are any diehards left, I throw out the clincher. "How many of you have goals for the next five years?" That's usually the eliminator.

Less than 5 percent of the population has a goal or plan for their lives. We *plan* business deals and vacation trips. We *plan* menus and shopping trips. We *drift* through life letting things "just happen." Then we complain, "I don't know what I want from life, but this certainly isn't it!"

Will a *laissez-faire* life-style be reflected on your epitaph: "She aimed at nothing and succeeded!"?

Dreams to Reality

Since our adoptions and the onset of my writing career I have been amazed at the number of people who respond sincerely with, "I've always wanted to adopt, but . . . " or "I've always thought I could write, but . . . " Dreams, wishes and fantasies but none turn into reality.

Visualize something you would really like to do. How about learning to play the piano? Becoming a gourmet cook? Teaching a Bible study? Learning to use a word processor?

Now close your eyes and visualize that dream accomplished—a reality. You are now sitting at the piano playing "My Tribute," serving a six-course French meal, leading a group at Bible Study Fellowship or earning a raise because of your new proficiency at the word processor.

By setting goals we can bridge the chasm between dreams and wishes, reality and accomplishment.

Many of us spend half our time working for things we could have if we didn't spend half our time wishing.

—Alexander Woollcott

What Is It?

Many people confuse goals and purposes. A purpose is a general statement. A goal is specific, attainable and can be measured by both action and date.

While my general purpose is to be a better Christian, my specific goal is to spend 30 minutes each morning in prayer and Bible study. That is specific, attainable and can be measured by both action and deed.

One of my long-term goals is to have three hours a day for prayer and Bible study (per Martin Luther). That's a great long-term goal, but unrealistic at this time.

In *Strategy for Living* the authors state, "A goal is a statement about how we hope things are going to be at some time in the future. A goal is a statement of faith, goals are statements about what we believe we need to do as well as what we need to be."[1]

Defined by Goals

Setting goals simplifies and defines our lives. Our choices, activities and our energies have a direction. If my goal is to have the cleanest kitchen in the world I will plan my life one way (and be very frustrated). If my goal is to create a warm, Christian home, I'll even decorate differently.

Even if I've invited guests for dinner I need to have a goal for the evening. If I want to impress Mrs. Barker with my culinary talents I'll plan a different menu than if my goal is to get to know the Barker family better.

Today we are confronted with a myriad of choices. "The confusion of having so many things to accomplish, so many directions in which to move becomes debilitating when there is no goal that gives flow and clarity to your activities."[2]

Winners

In studying goals I have found them to be a common link among high achievers. Charles A. Garfield, professor of psychology at the University of California, San Francisco Medical School, has studied over 1,200 "peak performers." He has found that they have several things in common:

1. They spend more than ²/₃ of their time doing things they choose to do and enjoy doing.
2. Commitment helps people know what tasks they want to do.
3. Goals are essential (goals and internal self-fulfillment).[3]

In her best-seller, *Pathfinders,* Gail Sheehy explores the secrets of well being and two quotes caught my attention because they confirm my belief in the importance of goal setting. "My life has meaning and direction" and "I have already attained several of my long-term goals that are important to me."[4]

And psychiatrist Ari Kiev of Cornell University writes,

In my practice as a psychiatrist I have found that helping people to develop personal goals has proven to be the most effective way to help them cope with problems. Observing the lives of people who have mastered adversity, I have noted that they have established goals and sought with all their effort to achieve them. From the moment they decided to concentrate all their energies on a specific objective, they began to surmount the most difficult odds . . . the establishment of a goal is the key to successful living.[5]

Opposition

In spite of all the evidence in favor of setting goals some people still object. Sigmund Freud discouraged goal setting because of the guilt that would follow when a goal was set and not met.

One respondent wrote,

Actually I find I shy away from most goal setting,

because I tend to suffer from disappointment if I don't reach my goal. If a goal is a promise to myself then broken promises are what disturb me the most, whether another promised me or I did. So I take the easy way out and don't promise . . . .

In spite of all the arguments we can come up with against goal setting I find I agree with Dr. Victor Frankl, "Not having a goal is more to be feared than not reaching a goal . . . . I would rather attempt to do something great and fail than attempt to do nothing and succeed."

Long and Short

We need to have a combination of long-range and short-range goals. The vision of a long-range goal can too often get lost in the "dailyness" of life. On the other hand, implementing some short-range goals can become tedious without the long-range vision beckoning before us.

One of my long-range goals is to create a loving Christian home for my family. The tediousness of scrubbing the bathroom or washing dishes can quickly wear me down if I don't have the long-range picture before me.

When my goal is sewing a dress, I don't always enjoy the sewing process, but the vision of a finished product keeps me going.

I am preparing a speech for a banquet later this month. My goal is to present that speech at a specific time and place and accomplish a certain purpose through my words. Standing in an empty room talking aloud makes me feel foolish (and the kids giggle), but I am looking forward to presenting the speech.

Bite Size

Another reason people often shy away from setting goals is the immensity of the goal. To avoid this we need to break goals up into manageable size portions. Some experts refer to this as the salami or elephant technique where you "eat" the whole thing one bite at a time.

When I picture cleaning our 15-room Victorian house I am

overwhelmed. When I break the job down room-by-room and list specifics under each room, the job is whittled down to a size I can handle.

Attainable

Goals need to be attainable. I was just given a writing assignment for an article on the church and persons with disabilities. My goal is to write that article. I have the expertise, contacts and resources to make that an attainable goal.

A friend of mine does profiles of sports figures. He is single, has the sports contacts and the flexibility to do the traveling. For him, it is an attainable assignment; for me, it wouldn't be.

If I'm interested in exercise, taking an aerobics class two nights a week might be an attainable goal; becoming a professional ballerina at my age would not be.

Stretching

It sounds contradictory, but we always need to include some goals that are personally stretching. By always having at least one goal that can't be accomplished without God's help, we will stretch and grow.

Dr. Robert Schuller challenges, "Let your goals become targets but never let them become ceilings. If your goals are not expandable they will be expendable."[6]

Whose Goal?

When you have set your goals go back over them asking, "Whose goal is this?" Make certain they are goals *you* want to set, not goals you feel pressured by other people to have.

Once we have set our goals (and ascertained they are ours) we also shouldn't compare them. A realistic goal for me might be out of the question for you. On the other hand what you can quickly and easily achieve might be totally unattainable for me. Set your individualized goals and don't compare.

I heard a story on the news one evening that illustrates this point perfectly. A girl ran in the New York Marathon. She had cerebral palsy and finished hours after the whole event was finished. There were no bands, lights or awards to meet her. Yet she was able to exult, "I feel good! I finished!" She had set her own personal goal and achieved it.

Once I taught a workshop and one 90-year-old lady obediently bought herself a notebook. I couldn't help but reflect that the notebook probably had more pages than she had days.

Mary set herself a goal to read through the Bible in the next year. She asked the nurses to leave her sitting up an extra hour each day and she carefully recorded her progress in a notebook. She followed the process perfectly and picked a goal that was attainable (yet stretching) for her.

Accountability

I write my goals in my prayer diary, to remind me to pray over my goals and also to remind me of my dependence on God.

It is also a good idea to verbally share them with a spouse or friend. Many goal-oriented couples set and review their goals together.

Karen warns,

> "When I first started setting goals I went over them with a friend. She brought perspective to my views, helped me be realistic and served as someone to whom I could be accountable. We haven't been able to get together as often this year and I have lost sight of the goal-setting process."

Review

In his book *How to Set Goals* Dr. Mark Lee writes:

> Goals must be verbalized, stated, and studied, and reviewed and amended. They are dynamic things, not static. They change, and change back again. Some are dropped, some become larger, and some introduce themselves late in the creative process.[7]

Review is necessary because life and goals are never static. In some areas our goals will remain basic; in other areas as our lives change so will our goals.

Count the Cost

As we set goals we need to be aware of their impact on our lives and be willing to count the cost. When a couple sets a goal that the wife will stay home full time until their children start school, that couple will be turning their back on other options. There will be a financial cost for that goal, but those costs are balanced by the rewards of giving those children a good start in life.

In *How to Take Charge* the authors warn,

To choose one goal means to give up others. If you affirm yourself in a certain way, that means you are turning your back on all other ways of being.
It means you can't have everything.
It means you can't do everything.
It means you can't be everything.
It means you can't please everybody.[8]

Enjoy the Process

I love to do needlework. When we first moved into this house with its twelve-foot high ceilings, I was inspired to cover the wall space. I raced through the first picture thinking only of my goal—the finished picture. When it was stretched and framed I looked closely at the picture. It was technically well done, but something was missing—the satisfaction I usually felt.

I realized that in my race to fill a space—to meet a goal—I had forgotten to enjoy the process. On the next piece of needlework I took time to enjoy watching the colors blend together and to savor the picture taking form. I enjoyed the process and had a deeper sense of satisfaction when the picture was eventually hung.

Too many times in life we rush through the days of childhood waiting to "have baby sleep through the night," or "I'll be so-o-o glad when she's out of diapers." Some parents wish away their children's whole childhood waiting for a better stage to arrive.

There are many journeys in life and few arrivals—take time to enjoy the trip along the way to reaching your goals.

HERE LIES

_____

SHE WAS COMMITTED
TO: _____

SHE ACCOMPLISHED:

_____

Goal-Setting Worksheet

1. What is my goal for today?

2. What is my goal for this week?

3. What is my goal for this month?

4. What is my goal for this year?

5. What are my long-range goals?

6. What dream would I like to see turned into reality?

7. What steps should I take to make that happen?

8. What areas of my life could be strengthened by using goals?

9. Who, besides God, will I be accountable to in my goal-setting?

10. What four Scripture references support my goals?

Goals

1. Set your goal.

2. Develop a plan to turn that goal into a reality.

3. Balance each day against these goals.

4. Present these goals to God:

    A. Spiritual Goal:

    B. Family Goal:

    C. Personal Goal:

    D. Professional Goal:

    E. Educational Goal:

    F. Marriage Goal:

When I am 65 I want to have:

> "Forgetting what is behind and straining toward what is ahead, I press on toward the goal to win the prize for which God has called me heavenward in Christ Jesus" (Phil. 3:13-14, *NIV*).

Goals: Turning Dreams into Reality

Dream

Goals

Congratulations

Chapter 14
Planning

"A man's heart plans his way, but the Lord directs his steps" (Prov. 16:9, *NKJV*).

A study in a leading women's magazine showed that women's most common time-wasting mistake was in trying to get everything accomplished without a strategy or plan.

In my workshops I have found that the few women who have set goals have also discovered the necessity of having a definite plan to work out those goals.

Planning is invested time. For each minute we spend in planning, we will save in the long run.

Consequences of Poor Planning

Bernard Baruch once said, "Whatever failures I have known, whatever errors I have committed, whatever follies I have witnessed in private and public life have been the consequences of action without thought."

And time management counselors warn that failure to plan is planning to fail.

> Failing to plan means that more and more valuable time is spent in putting out brush fires, coping with emergencies, being driven by events over which we have little control and for which we have not anticipated the coping strategies. This constant need to react to unrelenting impositions coming from the outside environment is yet another definition of stress.[1]

Planning Steps

Once we have set our goals, planning is the practical step that turns our goals into reality. Planning requires mental imagery, choices and action. Now walk through a planning session with me:

First, picture what it will take to accomplish a goal. I have a speaking engagement next month and my goal is to give an overview on time stewardship. I picture how I will look and sound (and I always picture a successful presentation and warm audience).

Second, list the choices to be made. Which form of presentation will be most effective? Should I use my audiovisuals? What will I wear?

Third, write out the steps of the plan:

    a. Prepare and study notes

    b. Update audiovisuals

    c. Check outfit, making sure it is cleaned, pressed and ready.

> Plan your work, work your plan

Planning Options

There are numerous ways to do daily planning. Several

companies offer excellent planners with space for things such as menus. Many executives use a leather covered daily planner with large calendar pages. Many homemakers run their domain from large calendars, using different colored pens for each family member.

Many of the women I know use a loose-leaf binder. Most agree on a 7 × 9-inch binder, although some of my friends who travel a great deal prefer a notebook even smaller that they can always carry in their purses.

With dividers and calendar pages you can set up the notebook whichever way helps you the most. Whatever form of daily planning you choose is not as important as making certain that you do choose one and use it with consistency.

Mae's Example

Mae is one of my more organized friends and once gave me a perfect example of how planning works in her life:

> I plan ahead so I'm not caught at the last minute with half a dozen things to be done all at once. Recently we had to have choir dresses made by a deadline, but before that I had several other activities. I took five minutes out and read the dress pattern to see how difficult it would be and decided I needed five hours.
>
> All the other things I took in order as they came along. When the day to sew came, it took the entire five hours, but I finished the dress on time.
>
> If I hadn't known how difficult it was going to be and not set aside the right amount of time, I'd never have made it because it was the day before the deadline.

Mae had a goal (making a dress) and she developed a plan (after studying the pattern). She followed her plan and in doing so she turned her goal into a reality. The principles of time stewardship really do work!

The Five W's of Planning

WHO . . . . will be best suited to do this?

WHAT . . . exactly am I planning?

WHEN . . . does this have to be finished? How much time do I need? How much can I accomplish in a given time?

WHY . . . am I doing this?

WHERE . . . is the best place to accomplish this?

Before you start your project go over each question.

After you finish the project go over each question for evaluation.

Chapter 15
Priorities

"But seek ye first the kingdom of God, and his righteousness; and all these things shall be added unto you" (Matt. 6:33, *KJV*).

Once we have set our goals and committed them unto God we need to set priorities—determine what is the most important thing at this time.

Pat King defines priority,

> Following Christ doesn't necessarily mean doing what looks right or what other people think is right. Instead it means discerning in my heart what I've been called to do and saying no to what I haven't been called to.[1]

Rev. Lloyd Ogilvie calls prioritizing "sanctified selectivity" and in a special issue of *Bostonia* they reported,

> The second issue in time management is the failure to set priorities. Some things are more important than other things. If we fail to ask, "Is this important?" we find ourselves skipping from one thing to another.[2]

ABC's

If we don't prioritize our goals first, we will get swamped when everything hits at once—and we're pulled in a dozen directions and don't know which way to go.

One of my goals is to take lessons to learn to use our microwave oven more efficiently. Another goal is to join a couple's Bible study with my husband.

When I prioritize my goals the Bible study has a higher priority than the microwave class. When I discover that the class is on the same night as the couple's Bible study, I know by my priorities which should come first.

When planning for the Bible study I know that I need to pick up two study books, call the leader to sign up for the class, find a baby-sitter and look at my schedule to see when I can study the weekly lessons.

After I have broken down the goal, I go back and assign priorities to each item:

> get two study books—C
> call leader to sign up—A
> line up baby-sitting—B
> look at schedule—D

Changes

Just like life, goals and priorities change and need to be periodically reviewed. At the end of June one of my goals is to have new school clothes ready by the start of school in September. By August 31 that job is either finished or becomes a very definite A-level goal. By being aware of the goal and its date I can avoid the panic of trying to shop for four children the week before school starts when the stores are jam-packed with other unorganized mothers.

Eliminating

Raising our adopted children with special needs and pursuing a writing career both require a lot of physical and emotional energy. When I prioritize my goals, break them down into steps and then prioritize the steps to reaching those goals, there are many things that don't make the list. I carefully examine what God wants me to do and say no to the rest.

Other People

At this point we need to be careful that we don't let other people's pressures come between us and what we believe God wants us to do.

The Sunday School superintendent's number one priority is finding qualified teachers. He approaches me with his priority list in hand—bump!

During the years we parented our foster child Melissa I wasn't able to assume that sort of outside responsibility. I had a strong sense of what God wanted me doing during that time and was able to say no to teaching a class without feeling guilty.

I did pray that just the right teacher would be found, and even if the Sunday School superintendent was disappointed in me, I had peace that I was doing God's will for me.

Individualized

Life is a constant series of choices and it can be totally overwhelming without goals and priorities to help us sort them out.

I have a friend who loves to work in her garden. Her flowers and vegetables bless many of us. She gives the inside of her house the old "lick and a promise" and hurries outside.

Considering the things I have to do, I realize that as much as I admire her yard, I can't put that many hours into yard work and still have the time and energy to accomplish those things on my priority list.

Each of us must pare our activities and responsibilities to fit our individual priorities. That means we are constantly sorting through activities with overall goals and specific goals in mind. This might mean cancelling subscriptions, resigning from a committee or scaling down our entertainment.

Choices

Those goals and priorities that we choose influence, shape and become part of our lives. The first year I attended a writer's conference I went with a friend. We were both seeking God's direction for our writing interests.

Four years later we compared notes. I was a published writer. She had finished college and was teaching children to write. Our lives were shaped by the goals we had set.

Dr. Anthony Compolo, a noted professor of sociology at Eastern College in Pennsylvania, says,

> What you commit yourself to be will change what you are and make you into a completely different person. Let me repeat that not the past, but the future, conditions you, because what you commit yourself to become determines what you are— more than anything that ever happened to you yesterday or the day before.
>
> And therefore I ask you a very simple question: What are your commitments? Where are you going? What are you going to be?[3]

Dr. Richard Halverson says, "Priorities are not just marginal options—they are life determining. One's personality is molded inescapably into the image of his priorities."[4] A writer, a gardener, and an English teacher—each molded by his/her personal goals and priorities.

Sorting

There are some questions developed by Engstrom and Dayton that we need to ask ourselves when sorting through priorities. I have applied these to everything from cleaning my house to taking on a new writing project.

1. How urgent is it?
2. How important is it?
3. How often must it be done?
4. Can someone *else* do it more effectively than I?
5. Is it part of the larger task or goal that I am committed to?
6. Is this the best way?[5]

In applying these questions I can better sort out things that I should be doing and things that can be eliminated, done by others, or touched on occasionally. If Becky's therapist asks me, for example, if I can do part of the therapy program at home I can go over the list and evaluate the situation: it is urgent, important, must be done daily, Dennis isn't available, it is part of a larger goal. I'll do it.

Shortly after I started using this checklist we had moved into our Victorian house with numerous doors (we're still counting). Each door has two ornate brass knobs and doorplates. One day my *thoughtful* husband bought me a can of brass polish and suggested I polish all those lovely old knobs.

To evaluate the brass polishing project I went down the list: it wasn't urgent, wasn't important (at least not to me) and someone else was welcome to do the job. If it had been more important to my husband, it could have fallen under question number five (and I'm *very* grateful that it didn't).

After I had used that illustration in several workshops I got curious one day and tried polishing and scrubbing one of those ornate knobs. Other than the strong smell of polish and an allergic headache I couldn't tell a difference between the polished knob and the others.

Dennis came home that evening and took one whiff, "Great! You did the knobs! They look terrific!"

The Five Year Test

Robin Worthington, writer, editor and mother of five, uses the five-year test to sort her priorities: "Will this matter in five years?"[6]

Shortly after she told me how she sorts her priorities one of our boys asked me to go watch his Little League game. There was still much housework to be done and I was torn between staying home to finish my work or going to the game. Robin's question came to mind: "Will this matter in five years?" I knew that in five years none of us would remember whether or not I had left dirty dinner dishes in the sink.

I went to the game.

Priorities Worksheet

List five of your goals. They need not be in any particular order.

1.
2.
3.
4.
5.

Now rank those goals by priority.

1.
2.
3.
4.
5.

List 10 things you have to do today.

1.
2.
3.
4.
5.
6.
7.
8.
9.
10.

Now prioritize each item on page 153 and assign an *A*, *B* or *C* rating (*A* being the most important).

PRIORITIES

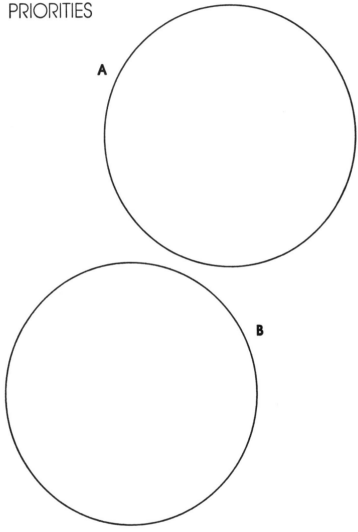

1. Circle *A* represents typical day.
2. Circle *B* represents an ideal day in five years.
3. What changes can I make now?
4. Can I live with the things I can't change?
5. In five years what will I wish I had done now?

Chapter 16
Decisions

"Multitudes, multitudes in the valley of decision!"
(Joel 3:14,*NKJV*).

Historically women have been "spared" a role in major decision-making. First, parents made the decisions, often including the choice of husband. Then the husband made all major decisions. Previous generations didn't even have the options we do for family planning.

Today more couples are sharing decisions, more women are single and forced to make all the family decisions and more women are working. For some, decision-making comes naturally; but for most of us, we feel like Joel who was trapped in the "valley of decision."

Decisions are part of almost every waking moment. Some are minor ones involving what color dress to wear, what to eat for breakfast and which route to take to work. Other decisions are life changing: "What do I want to do with my life? Do I marry him? When should we have children?"

Our work doesn't end once we've made a decision, for one decision always leads to others. No sooner have we decided we will have children and we're faced with a whole string of other decisions: How many? How far apart? Do I stay home or keep working?

A Difference

Once our family put itself under the Lordship of Jesus Christ, any decisions that we made took on a new dimension. The results seemed to have more eternal value and we felt a responsibility to God for those decisions. But along with the increased responsibility we also had new provisions—prayer and the Bible—to help us.

Throughout the first year that our whole family began loving and serving Jesus, I had a feeling of anticipation that there was something special in store for us. That something turned out to be adoption. Talk about heavy, life changing decisions! Here was one that would affect every aspect of all of our lives.

Once the decision was made to proceed with an adoption, we had to make specific decisions regarding a child. When that child was also black and had cerebral palsy the decision took on more significance and affected more people.

By bringing us through such momentous decisions early in our walk with Him, we were forced to learn some important steps.

The Process

When I first feel that God is leading in a certain direction, I pray about that impression on my own. If I'm still convinced of its worth, I then discuss it with my husband Dennis. If you're single, discuss your situation with someone that you're accountable to.

Dennis and I are a good balance. One of us is usually thinking with the mind while the other is feeling with the heart. We need both in decision-making.

After praying on my own and discussing the issue with Den-

nis, I make out a list and we go over it. My list is a simplistic out-
line of the pros and cons.

On the adoption list I wrote out all the positive results of
adding a fourth child to our family, including Scripture verses
about caring for orphans.

On the other side of the paper I listed all the negatives I
could possibly come up with including the reactions of other
people, finances and my physical limitations.

Together we went over the list item-by-item, choosing to be
more concerned about God's opinion than man's. I have, for
example, some trouble with my back and would be limited in
how much lifting I could do. Then we checked out what we
thought would be some financial negatives and discovered that
our state waives the fee for special needs adoptions and provides medical coverage. We also went over the effect this adoption would have on our other three children and spent many
hours in family discussion and private talks.

By the time we were through with the list there were many
more positives than negatives and we also felt peace in our
hearts about the decision.

It is important when using this list process that you go over it
with someone else. It's too easy to let our feelings influence our
thinking. As Gloria Gaither warns in her book *Decisions,*

> Whether we want to admit it or not, all our choices
> will ultimately be dictated by what we really want:
> *the strongest want will win.* We human beings can
> be very clever at conning ourselves. We can
> rationalize—even spiritualize almost anything. But,
> in the final analysis, what we think is most impor-
> tant is what we will choose, no matter what we tell
> ourselves or other people.[1]

Time Stealer

Decision-making can be a big energy and time stealer. After
a move to a new area we went out to dinner with another
couple in "unknown territory." We spent 45 minutes wander-
ing aimlessly asking, "What kind of food shall we eat? Italian?

Steak? Mexican?" Those 45 minutes that could have been more enjoyably spent in fellowship *inside* a restaurant were wasted because we were all too polite to make a decision.

Decision-making (or a lack thereof) can be a big energy and time stealer when:

- you can't decide what to do or what to do first;
- you make decisions too quickly or too slowly;
- you put off important decisions;
- you spend too much time agonizing or;
- worrying about low-priority decisions.[2]

Keeping these warnings in mind I try to cut out wasting time on decisions whenever possible. Before I go to bed at night I have planned what I will wear the next morning and what we will have for breakfast.

I used to start working in my office and waste precious time trying to decide where to start and what project to work on. Now the last thing I do before leaving my office is list what I'm to work on the next day. Established routine can help save decision time.

To Not Decide

Perhaps the person who floats through life without seeming to make any decisions has in reality made the biggest—to not assume responsibility but to give it over to others. There's a strange security in not deciding.

To not decide is to decide

When we were facing the very necessary decision of not keeping a troubled foster child I found myself staying out of the decision-making. Unconsciously I was trying to let the decisions be made by my husband and the social worker so I could avoid feeling guilty.

Decision is the logical follow-up to desire. In order

to cope with or handle a problem well, you must take control. To take control is to choose to make decisions. Too much of life is lived in indecision, which is really a decision in itself. Rather than living life on purpose, most people live by circumstances or by the decision of others.[3]

On-going Relationships

Too often we use a life-saver theology. When we are hard pressed for an important decision, we turn to God expecting immediate answers. Then after the decision is made we throw down the "life preserver" and go our way.

Lloyd Ogilvie emphasizes that making decisions should "flow out of a consistent, open, willing relationship with the Lord."[4] If we are out of consistent daily fellowship with God and then go to Him during emergencies for guidance, we are misusing God's resources.

All too often life-altering decisions are made in a frantic rush, without prayer or much thought. Gloria Gaither writes, "We all live at a breakneck pace these days. Time and circumstances push us all into a pressure cooker process of decision-making and keep us from approaching decisions with the Lord, prayer and a clear head."[5]

No matter how well thought out our decisions are there is always an element of risk. That's where we can exercise our faith—faith that we are making a right choice, then faith that even if we err God can still use our decision for our good and His glory.

Decisions Worksheet

Decision to be made: _____

Part A List everything that comes to mind for or against
this decision.

PRO	CON

Part B Go over this list and the following questions with your husband or someone that you're accountable to:

1. How will this decision affect my relationship with God?

2. How will this decision affect my family?

3. What Scripture references are appropriate to this decision?

4. Do I have inner peace about this decision?

5. Does this fit in with what I know about my spiritual gifts and temperaments?

6. Do I have confirmation from others?

7. What will I have to eliminate from my life with this decision?

8. What will be added to my life by this decision?

9. Can I honestly accept God's will in this matter?

10. How will this decision affect my time?

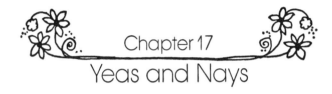

Chapter 17
Yeas and Nays

"Say just a simple 'Yes, I will' or 'No, I won't.' Your word is enough." (Matt. 5:37, *TLB*).

How often does our yes mean "Yes!"—spoken unreservedly with no strings attached? What other meanings are usually present in our answers?

"Yes" (but I really don't want to).

"Yes" (as long as I have the energy).

"Yes" (if I have time).

"Yes" (but I'll have to ask my husband).

Or we say yes fully suspecting that in a short time we will call and say, "I'm sorry, but . . . "

It is ironic that one of the first words we learn to say as children is the very word we have the most difficulty with as adults—no. I still remember the day my son, Tim, learned the power of that little word. For a whole day he used it for everything. By the end of the day he was a very hungry and thirsty little boy, but he had learned a very necessary lesson on the need to balance his yeas and nays. Unfortunately, that lesson learned by two-year-olds is too often forgotten by adults.

Problems and Possibilities

Whenever I cover this material on learning to say no I get more flak than any other subject I cover. The usual complaint is, "What will happen to the local church if everyone follows your advice and says no?"

Once I turned that question over to a pastor who was in the workshop. "What would happen to the local church if people only did what they felt God wanted them to do and said no to the rest?" The pastor seriously considered my question, and his face lit up with a beatific smile as he exclaimed, "If everyone in the church was doing what they truly felt God wanted them to be doing it would be the most dynamic, alive church possible!" He grinned through the rest of the class just thinking about the possibilities.

Respondents

Most of the respondents admitted to having a problem saying no. Reflected in the answers were only two groups of women who have learned to say no: the older women and the ones who have been forced by health limitations.

One woman wrote: "I had to take assertiveness training so I could say no and not feel guilty."

Darlene: "Sometimes as a single I'm overcommitted, but I feel I'm the only one to suffer. I need to learn to say no and not feel guilty. I don't want to miss anything, but I know it would be better for me and others if I did say no sometimes."

Marjorie: "I can say no to other people easier than to myself. I am an incorrigible hobbiest and an intriguing bit of needlework from the past claims my attention far easier than joining another group."

Allene: "I'm getting better. I've had to examine myself as to my reasons for taking on too much. Am I trying to get *my* needs met while pretending that I'm really meeting the needs of others? Am I saying to myself, 'You need me,' when what I really mean is, 'I need you'?"

WHY DO WE HAVE TROUBLE WITH NO?

Giving an appropriate no answer is a common problem for all of us. For Christian women the problem is compounded because we are often afraid that a negative answer will hurt our testimony.

Chuck Swindoll observes that where the Puritans once felt that cleanliness was next to godliness many people today sincerely identify fatigue with godliness. Why is the ability to give an *appropriate* no answer such a problem for us?

Self-Image

We worry that if we refuse their request other people won't like or respect us. We try to "buy" love and respect with yes answers.

As a young child I always felt that I had to prove my worth to others and this carried over into my adult life. For years I projected the messages "See how much I do?" and "See how often I say yes?"

The more healing we allow God to do of our self-image the better able we are to say yes because it's God's best for us, not because we are too insecure to say no.

Earned Love

Salvation is a gift of God, not something we have to earn, yet we often try to earn God's love and favor by *doing.*

One of the great liberating forces of my life has been the realization that nothing I can ever *do* will make God love me more than He does right this minute.

With that liberation I realize that often when we are afraid to tell someone no we aren't afraid of losing just that person's love and respect but also God's.

Losing Face

We all like to have people think well of us. Often we say yes to a doubtful task to save face and later use an excuse that puts the final decision outside of our control. That way we get credit for our willingness and the blame goes on someone else—"My husband just won't let me," "My doctor says I have to cut back," "My boss won't let me off."

Guilt

How many times have you take on a project not because you wanted to or felt you should, but because you felt so guilty about saying no?—"The cause is so worthy," "The chairman was so desperate for help," "But it seems so wrong to say no to the Lord's work."

Responsibility

We assume responsibility that is not ours when we feel that a project will fall through without our help. When I was forced by my health to resign all outside responsibilities for a few years I was surprised that the choir, Sunday School and Vacation Bible School all ran very well without me.

Too often we take on responsibility for God's reputation by thinking, "If I say no they will think poorly of Christians in general, God specifically."

Unrealistic Expectations

When we haven't studied ourselves and aren't aware of our spiritual gifts and temperaments or given thought to our physical limitations, we can easily have unrealistic expectations for ourselves.

For a brief time I enjoyed the Wonder Woman part that other people had scripted for me, but I almost did myself in trying to live up to that role. Part of the lesson that I learned during that time was to assess my time. When all six children were home, all had demanding special needs and we were averaging 30 doctor appointments a month. It was foolish to even think I could also handle a lot of outside responsibilities.

Decisions

We laugh at the stereotypical door-to-door salesman who thrusts his foot in the door trying to force a sale. How often have we given a spur-of-the-moment answer without going through the decision-making process?

WHAT ARE THE DANGERS?

Once we can recognize the reasons why we have so much trouble saying no we need to review the dangers.

Endangered Health

Over involvement takes a toll on our physical and mental health. Carol writes, "I became so overcommitted that I got sick and landed in the hospital. I was forced to take a good look at what got me there. I realized that I was physically overextended and that I'm not an indispensable person."

Stress and Burnout

Stress and burnout are epidemic today even among Christians—a painful consequence of not carefully weighing our yeas and nays. As Douglas J. Rumford says, "The late-date beatitude seems to be, 'Blessed are those who burn out, for they shall be comforted in Heaven.' "[1]

Loss of Joy

When we take on projects for the wrong reasons our joy in serving will often turn into resentment. John Dobbert warns, "When people consent to over involvement, invariably their attitude changes from one of joyous service to one of resentment as the rigorous schedule takes a toll on their physical and mental well-being."[2]

Lost Blessings

When we take on projects that God hasn't intended for us, we are guilty of robbing someone else of a blessing.

> Those assuming more than their share of responsibilities within the Body would be alarmed to know that they are performing a disservice to others within the fellowship. As they continue to say yes and accept additional responsibilities, regard-

less of the negative effects, others are deprived of service and the resulting fulfillment.[3]

Family Relationships

Family relationships can be destroyed by any type of over-commitment whether it be a job, ministry or service.

More churches are becoming aware of the need for family time, but ultimately it is our responsibility to guard that time.

What Message?

What message does our over involvement send out to the world? When friends and relatives who aren't Christian see us burned-out and stressed-out, what does that show them?

When we're never home or exhausted when we are, what are we "saying" to our children about service and stewardship?

In *Christianity Today* I read this warning,

> We need a balance between the ideal and the real, vision and actuality. It will mean determining and developing our spiritual gifts (nothing can burn us out faster than trying to accomplish a task for which we are not gifted), recognizing our limitations and (heresy of heresies in most circles) learning to say a gracious "no" when asked to do something that would cause us to overextend ourselves beyond our God-given capabilities. Through Christ we can do anything we ought to do. But it is precisely this misconceived *ought* that can make us overwrought and distraught.[4]

WHAT THE EXPERTS SAY

For the past few years I have been collecting what others have to say about the art of saying no. May we end this chapter with these gems from others:

Edwin Bliss: Of all the time-saving techniques ever developed, perhaps the most effective is the frequent use of the word no. You cannot protect your priorities unless you learn to decline, tactfully but firmly, every request that does not contribute to the achievement of your goals.[5]

Lloyd Ogilvie: All through the Lord's confrontation with the Pharisees we feel a kind of holy toughness about his response to their pressures to change and mold him. He exemplified his admonition that our yes be yes and our no be no (Matt. 5:37). It's a great sign of maturity to be able to say either decisively. It takes courage to say no to some of life's opportunities because, good as they may be, they may not be maximum for us.[6]

Howard Hendricks: A lot of people are defeated for the simple reason that they don't know how to say no. Does this help me to do what God wants me to do? No, it doesn't! Then friend, I eliminate it![7]

Charles Spurgeon: Learn to say no, it will be of more use to you than to be able to read Latin.

Dr. Gary Collins: The theology students in my classes have learned a lot about biblical language, but I try to convince them that there is one English word that is more important to them than all their Hebrew and Greek vocabulary put together. It's the word "no."[8]

Anne Ortlund: Under that wonderful umbrella of "if God wills," we need to decide where we suspect he'd like us to go. We need to see what provisions are necessary for each leg of the journey and get them. Then we need to say "no," "no," "no" daily all the rest of our lives to everything that would get us off course and keep returning and returning to our personal charts to make sure we're getting there.[9]

Gloria Gaither says it all in a song, "Yes to Something Higher":

> When you sense a calling that is the best that
> is within you,
> When you know deep in your heart you've
> found a better way,
> Turn your back on all the voices that would
> drag you downward:
> Saying "no" may be the grandest "yes" you'll
> ever say.[10]

Saying No Checklist

Except in rare cases do not give instant answers. Take time to pray and go over the checklists.

1. Have I gone over the decision checklist? (See chapter 16.)

2. Have I prayed over this decision?

3. If I say yes, will this fit with my goals and time schedule?

4. Do I really feel this is part of God's plan for me?

5. Exactly why am I going to say yes or no?

"Lord, help me to realize how brief my time on earth will be. Help me to know that I am here for but a moment more. My life is no longer than my hand! My whole lifetime is but a moment to you. Proud man! Frail as breath! A shadow! And all his busy rushing ends in nothing."

(Ps. 39:4-6, *TLB*).

Chapter 18
Scheduling

Mention "schedules" and the grumbling starts. "They're too restrictive," "I don't want to be tied to one of those things," "Can't there be any spontaneity in my life?," "Schedules? Never!"

I used to share some of those reservations, but when we had three small children I started to see the necessity of regular nap and feeding times. Then when we adopted Becky and Benji I quickly discovered that each child adjusted more smoothly when we followed through with the same schedule and routine that they were used to.

For years now I have been forced to adhere to a schedule: bus schedules, one of the children gets sick whenever she's up past 10 o'clock, routine doctor and therapy appointments. While sometimes it is restrictive, I have seen many positive benefits from regular scheduling.

When I started writing professionally I sat down and did my first half hour by half hour schedule to see if there was any possible time where I could have two uninterrupted hours. Only by going over each detail of my schedule was I able to find the necessary two hours. I've been a believer in schedules ever since.

Others Say—

Many women shared their views on scheduling:

Marsha: "My biggest time challenge is me! I am more than moderately rebellious and I deeply resent a piece of paper (schedule) governing my days and weeks. I know in my mind that if I write the schedule I am in control, but I still rebel. I keep telling the Lord He's in control and then taking it back again."

Joy: "As a pastor's wife I can't function without my schedule, yet I maintain flexibility."

Carla: "As a busy mother of 12 I have to schedule meetings and appointments first and then see when I can sew, cook, go to lunch, study, etc."

Marjorie: "Giving my schedule to the Lord involves three things: (1) My emotions—I must sincerely want to change; (2) My will—I must commit myself to God's guidance and use that schedule; and (3) My time—It's really His and I have to acknowledge that and allow Him to have a closer hand in all I do. All of this sounds great, but doing it—there's the rub! I'm glad I have the power of the Holy Spirit both to 'will and to do.'"

And in her book, *The Creative Homemaker,* Mary Bouma says,

> When I did not have my time organized my chores ran me; now I can master them. I thought a schedule would be arbitrary and restrictive, but it has turned out to be quite the opposite. It can give freedom. God is a God of order and He seems to use us and our talents in an orderly fashion.[1]

The Need

Whether we acknowledge it or not there is a recognized need in our lives for order and scheduling. Steve Douglas warns, "Many of us live in the dream world of what we intend to do and keeping a schedule helps us come to grips with the reality of what we can do."[2]

In an interview in *Leadership,* time management expert Ed Dayton was asked, "What is the best motivation to help people do something about controlling their schedules?" Mr. Dayton replied,

> First, discontent. You must get to the place where you are sick and tired of living a hectic life. Second, prayer. Do what we call fantasizing in prayer. Get away for a day alone somewhere. Bring yourself into God's presence and think about what kind of life you'd like to have 15 years from now. Picture in your mind a day in your life. What would you like to do on a typical day 15 years from now?[3]

One of the tools used to treat patients suffering from depression is scheduling. "God Himself plans and schedules; you, who are created in His image, cannot do without the order that scheduling brings."[4]

Times of Stress

When our weekly doctor-therapy appointments were at their maximum there were days that were impossible to schedule well despite my best efforts. Those days were committed to the Lord and I agreed with Charlie Shedd, "There are no places, no time-crannies where the Spirit of Christ cannot permeate to bless, provided we let Him be Lord of every minute."[5]

Once I was able to allow God to "permeate" every minute the frustration level of these uncontrollable days has been drastically reduced.

When I am going through an interval of constant stress (new child, surgery, prolonged illness) I review and revise my schedule to relieve any stress possible.

In an article on "Coping with Stress" I read,

> Effective time management and the ability to organize one's life events are important ingredients

in the management of stress. People who are chronically overcommitted and unable to maintain any kind of schedule in their daily lives are likely to feel they are getting nothing done at all. This leads to frustration, anger, a sense of helplessness and depression. Without a daily schedule, many people are unaware of what needs to be done in any given time period.[6]

And Susan Issacs recommends,

If you feel overwhelmed, make a list of all the things you must accomplish and then schedule them on various days in the next week. They can't all get done at once and going over them mentally without scheduling them simply causes more stress.[7]

First Step

When scheduling was brand new to me I started by keeping a detailed listing of all the activities for at least a week. By doing this I was able to see patterns, strengths, weak spots and any spare moments.

This initial round with scheduling should include *every* single thing that you do. You want to get very well acquainted with what fills your days.

After you have filled a week's worth of schedules, go over the schedules and make one schedule that represents an *average* day.

Now thoroughly examine this average schedule: How much am I actually accomplishing? Am I taking advantage of my prime time? How does this schedule reflect my goals? How does it reflect my walk with Christ?

Now take out a clean schedule and we will start letting our schedule be a positive aspect of our lives.

WHAT GOES ON A SCHEDULE?

Now that we have gone over some of the reasons for using

a schedule and seen how scheduling can relieve stress, we come to the question of what actually goes on a schedule.

There are some basic questions we need to ask before anything gets written on our schedule:

- Does the Lord want this?
- How will this affect my family?
- What will I have to take out of my schedule to fit this in?
- Why do I do this activity? Could someone else do this?
- What do I really want from life?
- At this rate where will I be in 5, 10, 15 years?
- Is this schedule helping me toward my goals?

God First

The first thing I put on my schedule is my devotion time. At this point I like to then pray over my schedule and commit it to God. I ask His guidance as I fill it in, I ask His blessing, and I ask for His help in areas that are a problem.

Can't Control

Next I fill in those things that I really can't control: bus schedules for the children, routine doctor or therapy appointments, any hours I'm working outside the home, church and Bible study.

Reflecting Your Goals?

Whenever possible I try to pad my schedule for some very necessary flexibility. Go over your goals as you schedule your time and make certain they are reflected here. Do I have time with my husband? Time for exercise and relaxation? Time for friends? Time for myself?

Routine

What routine things need to be scheduled in? Cleaning, shopping, errands? I use my schedule to plan my daily menus.

If I see I won't be home from the doctor until late on Tuesday I plan a quick meal. On the days when my schedule is freer I plan more complicated dishes.

Prime Time

I look for any uninterrupted time to fit in my writing. For you this might be study time, sewing time, craft time—any project that requires quality, uninterrupted time.

I know I'm not a night person so any projects that require heavy concentration will be scheduled earlier in the day.

Rest Time

When I was recovering from surgery I scheduled an afternoon rest as a necessity. Anne and Doris have chronic health problems and their rest time is a daily necessity.

Rewards

When I look over my weekly schedule and see that I have a very busy week ahead of me I often deliberately pile up on one day to create a "free day." Especially when I have been going through one of life's rougher periods this is a great help for me.

If every day is packed with appointments (a periodic happening around here), I will rearrange things and create one free day at home. Having this to look forward to helps me through the other days.

Impressions

> I find that the best way to handle impressions is first to make sure that I am always walking in the Spirit. Then, when I am impressed to veer from my schedule in some way, I simply pray and ask God to confirm that the impression is really from Him.[8]

I had read this statement and tried to implement Steve Douglas's recommendation when one day a friend asked, "I'm supposed to speak at a rally and you have more experience, will you do it?"

I knew my immediate schedule held a book deadline but agreed to pray about my answer. After prayer, I still felt the strong impression that I should stick to my schedule. When I gave my friend my answer she replied, "I got the same impression and I realized I was trying to give away a blessing God had in store for me."

If I had not taken time to listen I would have robbed my friend of a blessing and myself of needed writing time.

Looser Schedule

I kept a detailed schedule until I got a "feel" for my time. Now I use calendar pages rather than half-hour blocks. I have enough of a feel for my schedule and I can now fit things within that framework.

Review

About twice a year I fill out a detailed schedule and go over it item-by-item. I use this when my life undergoes a change (beginning of school year, summer, other major time changes). I also go back to the detailed schedule if I find the important things being crowded out.

When I review my schedule I jot down comments about what I did—was that meeting last week productive or a waste of time? Am I working toward my goals? What patterns do I see? What changes need to be made? What hidden bits of time can I use?

> "I recommend you take care of the minutes, for the hours will take care of themselves."
> —Chesterfield

Daily Schedule

Use this as a model. Keep a schedule for one week, then make up an average schedule. Analyze each entry in your average schedule. Set up a model schedule and record your actual daily schedule. Measure your schedule against your goals.

5:30 A.M.	
6:00	
6:30	
7:00	
7:30	
8:00	
8:30	
9:00	
9:30	
10:00	
10:30	
11:00	
11:30	
12:00	
12:30	
1:00 P.M.	
1:30	
2:00	
2:30	
3:00	
3:30	
4:00	
4:30	
5:00	

5:30	
6:00	
6:30	
7:00	
7:30	
8:00	
8:30	
9:00	
9:30	
10:00	
10:30	
11:00	
11:30	
12:00	

I've only just a minute
Only 60 seconds in it
Forced upon me—can't refuse it
Didn't seek it didn't choose it
But it's up to me to use it
Give account if I abuse it
Just a tiny little minute
But eternity is in it.

—Anonymous

Chapter 19

Interruptions

"But Jesus was sleeping. The disciples went and woke him, saying, 'Lord, save us! We're going to drown!' . . . Then he got up and rebuked the winds and the waves, and it was completely calm" (Matt. 8:24-26, *NIV*).

Interruptions. Part of life. Time wasters. Blessings in disguise. Interruptions can range from the trivial and unimportant to the life changing—from the unnecessary fifth drink of water at bedtime to a broken-hearted friend.

For years many of the interruptions in my life have been of small child variety: "Just one more drink!" "Can I make cookies? I promise I'll clean up!" "Mom! Tim just bled all over the carpet!" The average manager is interrupted an average of eight times an hour. While no such figure is available for mothers, it has been 21 years since I have finished a complete sentence.

Discernment

How do we discern what is important and what is a trivial distraction? There are two basic essentials for interruption control: establishing priorities and surrendering every day to the Lord.

Once we establish priorities we have a standard of measurement for each thing that comes into our lives. So often life is like a teeter-totter: a delicate balance between choices. This balancing act is seldom more evident than in our handling of interruptions.

When I first started giving every part of every day to the Lord, I was amazed at how the interruptions seemed to mostly filter away and what was left was what God wanted in my life.

Correspondents

The correspondents had some good perspectives on the subject of interruptions:

Pat: "When I pre-pray my day interruptions don't cause frustration. Remembering that people are more important than projects helps keep interruptions from causing problems."

Kathy: "I figure out my most productive times of least interruption and do high concentration things then."

Darlene: "I try to accept them as from God, but it isn't always easy. Somehow the Lord has a way of helping me do what is really necessary in spite of interruptions."

My favorite was from 73-year-old Mary: "I keep my purse and car keys handy by the door and say, 'I'm just on my way out!' Then I bolt away for brief (but necessary) errands instead of having time wasted with salespeople, nothing-else-to-do visitors or drop-ins who disregard my work schedule."

Sometimes No

In *How to Handle Pressure* the author warns,

Satan will sidetrack you if he can. If he can trick

you into thinking that a distraction is really your primary function, he will have led you on a detour far from God's main track for your life. Or he may get you involved with so many secondary influences (all kinds of distractions) that you don't have time to do God's will. If Satan can't get you in this way he'll try to cause you to become uptight and disagreeable about interruptions and people who cause them. Then to top it off, he'll weigh you down with a load of pressure because you're behind in your work.[1]

A new family moved onto our block and I wanted to show my neighborliness, Christian love, and witness to them about Jesus. I took over some homemade cookies and gave the busy mother my phone number.

Annie had my number memorized by the end of the first week—just by sheer usage. Moving from one crisis to another, she had more illnesses, injuries and family emergencies in a week than most of us have in a lifetime.

I was under the impression that to witness to her I had to be at her constant beck and call. After each call and plea for help I would smile outwardly and mumble, "This is for the Lord."

After knowing Annie for one month I sat down and took inventory of my life: my house was a mess—I had just cleaned Annie's; my dinner was late—I had just fixed Annie's; my kids were feeling neglected—I was tired out from Annie's.

I knew I couldn't keep up the pace of the past few weeks, but I was still concerned about my plan to witness to Annie. In desperation I talked with our pastor. "Your first priority is your own family," he reminded me. "As long as you can take care of them and help your neighbor, that's fine. But when your family is neglected it's going too far."

When I read the warnings found in *How to Handle Pressure,* I understood the process I had gone through. I was becoming uptight about Annie's constant demands and feeling the pressure of being behind in my family responsibilities.

I prayed about my contacts with Annie. I made a point of

seeing her for coffee and trying to maintain the relationship but started turning down many of her demands. Some interruptions are not exactly heaven-sent.

Handling Catastrophic Change

Some interruptions such as divorce, death, moving and illness are life changing. Again the respondents offered advice on how to cope with catastrophic change:

Allene: "Whenever there are major changes that I can have some control over I try to schedule them during a slow time or make a slow time. I planned a recent move before I started school and I took off time when my father died."

Karen: "I've learned the stages of grief. I can recognize them and I've given myself permission to cry, to feel angry. An old man once said that his favorite verse was, ' . . . and it came to pass . . . ' Why? Because it didn't come to stay. All things eventually change."

Kathy: "I recently moved and I'm realizing that it takes time to settle in. I just flex and realize things will get better and God has a plan."

Carla: "My husband and I write down the positive and negative aspects of new situations and have a family meeting to explain the circumstances and make necessary adjustments."

Mary: "When my husband died I had to take time off to just coast mentally and emotionally."

Virginia: "I tackle the worst things first and just take one day at a time."

Anne: "The big interruptions come in my life as a result of my chronic health problems. The only way I can handle this is to wait until I'm feeling well enough to regroup and start over."

Patterns

We were discussing interruptions in one of my workshops and Lisa complained that her children always interrupt when she's sewing. When we discovered that Lisa did her sewing between 3:00 and 5:00 each afternoon (as children troop home from school), it was suggested that she review her schedule and find another time for sewing.

Lisa's situation brings out a good point: Is what we perceive as an interruption possibly bad timing on our part? There are numerous chores that Lisa could do during that time period that would make her more accessible to her children.

When interruptions occur on a frequent basis, we need to review the situation and see what we can do to lessen the problem.

Buying Time

One of the most valuable commodities for women is uninterrupted time. It's not only valuable but hard to come by.

Busy women have found numerous ways to "buy" this quality time:

- put a "do not disturb" sign on your door;
- unplug the telephone or invest in an answering machine;
- set the timer and ask young children to play quietly until the timer goes off;
- borrow the home of a friend whose house is empty during the day;
- go to the mountains or a park for the day;
- make others aware of an uninterrupted time frame you need for resting or studying;
- make a baby-sitting trade with another friend who has young children.

Importance

Dietrich Bonhoeffer once said,

We must be ready to allow ourselves to be interrupted by God. God will be constantly crossing our paths and cancelling our plans by sending us people with claims and petitions. We may pass them by, preoccupied with our more important tasks.

Late one afternoon I heard the shrill noise signaling that my daughter's bus had arrived. We were moving and I had last-minute packing and dinner to fix before my husband arrived with the moving van.

I dashed out to get my daughter, intent on the chores waiting for me inside. The driver wanted to talk—and talk. I hadn't really cued in on what she was saying because my mind was so occupied by the *important* things waiting to be done.

When I noticed the driver had tears in her eyes I finally started listening. "My mother just died and if only the service had been in a church I could have accepted God because I know I need Him."

By this time she had my full attention and I told her how to accept Jesus as her personal Saviour. What I originally perceived as an interruption was one of God's opportunities.

Interruption Checklist

1. When am I most often interrupted?

2. Is there a pattern to my interruptions?

3. What steps can I take to control some interruptions?

4. Can I turn interruptions over to God? How?

5. Find five examples of how Jesus handled the interruptions of His life.

Lost, yesterday, somewhere between
    sunrise and sunset, two golden hours,
    each set with sixty diamond minutes.
    No reward is offered, for they are gone
    forever.

—Horace Mann

Time Thefts

Time Thieves	Problem for me	Within my control	Out of my control
Poor Communication			
Waiting			
Overload			
Poor sense of time frames			
Procrastination			
Unclear goals and priorities			
Failure to delegate			
Blame shifting			
Committee meetings			
Telephone			
Interruptions			
Can't say no			
Poor habits			
Paperwork			
Worry			
Guilt			
Reading			
Fatigue			
Television			
Sleeping late			
Junk mail			
Arguing			
Comparison			
Lack of concentration			
Poor planning and scheduling			

Go over the above time thieves and ask: Is this a problem for me? If you answer yes, then ask: Is this within my control or is this out of my control?

Go back over any that you checked as "out of your control" and carefully examine these to see if you are blaming external causes (others) for an internal problem (yourself).

Adapted from a University of California Extension Worksheet

Martha's Time-Saver Primer

"Reverence for God adds hours to each day"
(Prov. 10:27, *TLB*).

This is the section our friend, Martha, would be most pleased with: a collection of time-saving tips.

Accumulate

Dr. Dobson once said, "A household can be managed; it is the accumulating projects that break our backs." With this in mind train your family with the simple axiom, "If you use it put it away."[1] This system will keep clean-up chores from accumulating around the house.

Aftermath

In training children to be responsible it is often necessary to allow them to reap the consequences of their behavior: homework left at home, baseball glove at Steve's house, no lunch. Coping with the aftermath often helps break the cycle for habitual forgetters.

Automobile

Pat is a busy suburban mother who logs in many hours in transit. "I keep a 'flight plan' posted on the dashboard. The errands are listed in geographical order and the time of any appointments is also listed. All you have to do is leave one child behind somewhere to see the importance of this."

When I have errands around town I use those little sticky notes to list where I have to go. Rather than take time out of each day I will often save errands for one time block.

For traveling out of town I have a small clipboard on the seat beside me. I have a map and/or directions, name, address and phone number of where I'm going.

Barter

If there are certain chores you don't like, barter with your husband and children. Trade one of their least favorite chores for a job you don't relish.

Bathrooms

Assess the bathrooms in your home: (1) Are they easily cleaned? (2) Are there duplicate supplies in each bathroom? (3) Is there a container for tub toys?

Bedrooms

With a notebook in hand assess each bedroom: (1) Are things stored in the bedroom that could be stored elsewhere? (2) What would make this room easier to clean? (3) Can the children reach the storage space in the room? Can they reach the closet rods? Is there a study place? (4) What atmosphere do I want to achieve in the master bedroom? Is there adequate light for reading? Does this room have the ambiance of a retreat from the world?

Bulletin Board

Bulletin boards are used to keep track of family activities. Post notes to other family members informing them of Little League schedules, school lunch menus, etc.

Calendars

I love 'em! Purse size, giant year-at-a-glance size, one-day-at-a-time size. Try using a different colored pen for each family member's activities.

Darlene: "A calendar is *very* important to me. Does that mean the memory starts to diminish after 40?"

Catalogues

Do as much shopping as possible through the catalogues. Catalogues save time, gas and money.

Child Labor Questions

1. Am I allowing for mistakes?
2. Am I willing to compromise?
3. Do I respect their schedules?
4. Do I let them have some fun work?

Children

Peg Bracken says that we don't keep house for our children but in spite of them. We need to find a system that works for our family for encouraging children to help more. The respondents reported various ways of encouraging this help:

Merri: "Early in the week my son is told what must be done on Saturday and he knows not to make any plans until those chores are done."

Dorothy: "I tried a variety of things that changed as the children grew. I always felt it was important to praise a child in the help they did give."

Gloria: "Since we work for them we need their help. So no

allowance for chores but much praise and appreciation."

Darlene: "Before I went to work I shared that my teaching at the Christian school would be a ministry and that by helping they would be part of that ministry too."

Phyllis: "It was a difficult adjustment for me to accept their help without feeling guilty about me not doing *my* job. I've had to learn to accept a standard of neatness that's a little lower than I would do myself."

Regina: "Our children were expected to do certain assigned chores. If I inspected the job and found it hadn't been done I would go to them and bring them home to finish the job—from the football field, Little League game, friend's home. It usually only took one or two times to make my point."

Communication

Need more help? Communicate your needs. Often husbands and children are so programmed to having us do all the housework that they don't realize the extra pressures of small children or a job outside the home. Communicate your needs in a calm non-threatening way.

Comparison

"Her house is cleaner," "Her children help more," "She has a maid," "Her husband helps." The opportunities for comparison are endless and time consuming.

As Robin Worthington says, "When someone else is doing more than you, don't hate 'em, just let 'em. If you try to keep up with them you'll just be a fatigued imitation."[3]

When we seek to know and do the Father's will, comparisons should cease.

Do-It-Yourself

There are many excellent do-it-yourselfers, but there are times when hiring a professional is a time (and money) saver. Darlene reports that her worst time mistakes are do-it-yourself projects. "I end up spending more money and time correcting my mistakes than if I'd paid to have it done professionally."

Doubletime

As with the widow's mite it isn't the size but the commitment. So it is with little mites of time. Hand sewing can be done while watching TV; a long cord on the kitchen phone allows flexibility to work and chat. Make a game of trying to do two things at once.

Drawers and Closets

Go through every drawer and closet in the house. If you haven't used it in a year, throw it out. (Don't forget Goodwill and garage sales.)

For little used items (Christmas decorations, etc.) have a method of recording what and where each is stored.

Errands

Save one day to run errands. Plan your route to run errands in geographical order. This will save both time and gas.

Excellence

Excellence is attainable, gratifying and healthy. Perfection is unattainable, frustrating and neurotic. It's also a terrible waster of time.[4]

Favorite Time Savers

Carla: "Train children to help with grocery shopping."

Pam: "I do double cooking: one for dinner and one for the freezer."

Susan: "I clean the space I'm in to avoid cleaning all day Saturday."

Linda: "I buy gifts all year round so I can avoid big shopping trips."

Karen: "I try to do related things together so that I don't

have to keep coming back to the same tasks."

Susie: "The microwave isn't the answer to all the world's problems, but with two children eight months apart it is the nicest tool to come along."

Gloria: "I'm working out the saying, 'If you use it put it away.' There are days at our house where I think if this were done I would save at least 30 years."

File Cards

Karen's favorite time saver is a file box:

> I have an extra long file box that holds 3×5-inch cards. There are dividers for addresses and phone numbers; monthly dividers for information I'll need as each month comes up.
>
> I have sections for recipes; finances (listing policy and account numbers); a health section that has one card per person with health history; menu sections with everyone's favorite; family section with everyone's birthdates, special interests and current sizes.

File System

Develop a home filing system that meets your needs. Use a filing cabinet or cardboard file boxes. File insurance papers, school reports, warranties, magazine articles you want to read later, decorating tips, fashion and beauty ideas and Bible study notes.

Friends

Going through a busy time when your schedule and your friends' seldom mesh? Keep a supply of cute cards and send frequent notes; use the telephone to keep in touch. During one long siege of doctor and therapy appointments I invited a neglected friend to go with me. She went with me on many of the appointments and we did our weekly shopping together. It wasn't as good as a long visit over a pot of tea, but it did help our relationship survive the siege.

Gear-Shifting

In *Napa Outlook* they warn against "gear-shifting." Try to group related activities together. This approach helps prevent the time wasting gear-shifting that occurs when we go back and forth from totally unrelated activities.

Glove Compartment

Few things are more frustrating and time wasting than being stuck in a car without necessities. Keep your glove compartment emergency ready. Have coins for tolls and phone calls; Kleenex and moist towelettes; a map; a flashlight with fresh batteries; and an SOS tag for your antenna.

Granny's Schedule

I suspect my granny instinctively knew about gear-shifting: most of our grandmothers had their weekly chores planned out by schedules. A baking day, wash day, etc. This isn't always feasible today, but try to develop a system that works for you. Take your schedule sheet and plug in household chores.

Halo

Christopher Fry once said, "What, after all, is a halo? It's only one more thing to keep clean." Trying to earn a halo for being wonderwoman can be hazardous to your health.

Home

A counselor once told me, "You can tell the state of a woman's mind by the state of her house." We need to keep a balance between compulsive and comfortable. Winston Churchill observed, "We shape our homes, then our homes shape us." Question for the day: How is my home shaping me?

House Tour

With pad and pencil in hand go through your house and take inventory, itemizing all furniture and valuables for insurance purposes, cleaning and repair work and future purchases. Also ask yourself as you enter each room, "What would make this area easier to clean and enjoy?"

Husbands

Nothing can help us save more time than a helpful husband. When asked how much their husbands helped the respondents in the younger age brackets reported receiving quite a bit of help from their husbands. A few older women reported, "He's been helping some in the past few years." A large percentage replied that their husbands are very helpful "if I ask." And one respondent merely wrote, "chuckle!"

Ice

Have a few extra minutes? Fill up your ice trays and later in the day put the cubes in a plastic bag. Stash it away in the back of your freezer for use during one of those hot days when there's never enough ice.

Now look around the kitchen—what other jobs can you do in a short time and that will be of help sometime in the future? Clean a cupboard? Sort the spices?

Important Jobs

Instead of spending an entire weekend tackling a big important job spend a few minutes every day on one of these monsters. Have a list (from your inventory) of big time-consuming jobs and save them for those bits of time when there are willing bodies, extra time and energy.

Inventory

Go through the house (especially storage areas) with organization and time saving in mind. Make notes on every area that could be improved, then develop a plan of attack (also see *House Tour*).

Jawbone

How much time did I waste today in unnecessary chatter?

Jeopardy

Ready for another tour of your house? This time take a safety tour of your house. Check for fire hazards and fire exits. Plan a family fire drill. Make note of dark stairs and things that can be easily tripped over. Remove poisons and electrical dangers.

Jot

One way to save time is to jot down *everything* we do and analyze our use of time. An amazing amount of bits and pieces of time can be found this way. Things we often aren't even aware of often take up valuable time—like reading a magazine you intended to put away or watching half a TV program when you meant to turn it off.

Kids

Establish a routine and let your kids know what is expected from them. In *When Mom Goes to Work* Mary Beth Moster warns, "Remember it's not what you expect from your children, it's what you *inspect* that will get done."[5]

Phyllis Diller wisely cracks, "Cleaning your house while your kids are still growing is like shoveling the walk before it stops snowing."

Kill Time and You Murder Opportunity

Kitchen

With a note pad in hand, evaluate your kitchen by asking:
1. Am I organized for maximum efficiency?
2. Are things stored near where they're used?
3. Is this room easy to clean?
4. Are there things in here I seldom use? If so, give them the one year test. If it's an item needed but seldom used, can I store it elsewhere?
5. Put this motto in your kitchen—"If you use it, clean it and put it away."

Lists

If a brisk wind whipped through our house and blew my lists away I would be lost. Totally. Not only do "to-do" lists make things more manageable but counselors frequently use lists in helping patients with depression.

Janet keeps herself supplied with plain sheets of paper. She keeps them loose on her desk so they can be thrown away when the chore is done. There is something emotionally satisfying in this—"I love to crumple them up and start a fresh, clean page," Janet writes. The psychological term for the sense of well-being Janet gets from a finished list is "closure."

Dianne receives a great deal of help from her lists. "There's a feeling of accomplishment with each item crossed off. I've been blessed with a great memory—only it's extremely short—so I write everything down!"

> The Dullest Pencil Has a Better Memory than the Sharpest Mind

Living Room

Analyze this room: Do we use it for games, reading, television, entertaining? Review each use and make certain the room is arranged suitably for those activities. What does this room say about you and your family to a first-time visitor?

Mail

When I go to the post office each day, I sort through the mail and toss all junk mail away. When I bring the daily mail home, I sort it: magazines to the reader's room, bills in their special place. I read letters and save personal ones to answer in one sitting.

Memos

Establish a central place to post family notes. Bulletin boards work for these but many of us use the front of the refrigerator. (If you have teens, that's one place you can count on them looking.)

Night Before

1. Plan ahead by setting out everyone's clothes and setting the breakfast table before going to bed.
2. Cook company meals in advance.
3. Get adequate rest.

Notebooks

Merri wrote, "My number one time-saving tool is a notebook that has my whole life in it."

I use a variety of notebooks around the house. In the kitchen I have a 7×9-inch one that has a running grocery list, the family's favorite meals, menu suggestions and what I served company and when.

My cookbooks are numbered so if Robby's favorite meal

features chicken rolls, I'll jot down 3-42 in my notebook. I know that means cookbook number 3, page 42. If there is no number listed that means it's a recipe I know or is in my recipe box.

I also use a budget notebook, a moving notebook (when appropriate) and a decorating notebook where I file pictures and ideas I hope to try.

John Wesley is said to have kept his daily schedule in a little black book. Someone once asked him what he would do if he knew this were to be his last day on earth. Without batting an eyelash he replied, "Let me look at my little black book and I'll tell you."

Office Space

My favorite tool for organization is having a personal office space. This can range from one drawer in the kitchen to a corner of a bedroom, a converted closet or a whole room. I've used them all.

Set up your office space, then develop a filing system that fits your needs. Keep the system as simple as possible; don't make one so complicated that you end up tied to it.

Bank of America offers a free booklet on personal record keeping that is excellent:

Specialized Services #3401
Bank of America
P.O. Box 37128
San Francisco, CA 94137

Ask for "Consumer Information Report #21—Personal Record Keeping."

Paperwork

Everyone complains of getting bogged down with paperwork. The standard recommendation is to handle paperwork only once.

Positive Reinforcement

My grandmother would have called it bribery; today it's known as positive reinforcement. When the sun is shining and the flowers start blooming and I don't want to stay inside and work, I find little treats to nudge me along.

After I clean the kitchen I can sit down with a cup of tea; when the ironing is done, I can go pick some flowers; and at the end of this chapter I will go for a walk.

Prime Time

Once you discover when your prime time is, use it carefully. "If the hourly cost of your time works out to $25.00, then the hourly cost of your prime time will be closer to $50.00. You just don't spend $50.00 to straighten a desk drawer or open mail."[6]

Proscrastination

Procrastination is one of the most publicized time wasters. Of all the descriptions of procrastination I have read, my favorite is from Chuck Swindoll:

> His name? Procrastination. His specialty? Stealing time and incentive. Like the proverbial packrat, he makes off with priceless valuables, leaving cheap substitutes in their place: excuses, rationalizations, empty promises, embarrassment and guilt.[7]

During the next week whenever you put off doing something you know you should be doing, stop and analyze what you're feeling and get to the root cause of your procrastination.

Questions

Whenever you start to do routine chores, stop and question what you are doing: Does this job have to be done? Is there a better, faster way? Can someone else do this job? Why am I doing this job this particular way?

Queue

Always be prepared for waiting. With a small notebook in your purse and a pocket-size Bible you are always prepared to occupy your time while waiting. I have a few postcards in my purse notebook and even standing in a bank line I can write a postcard or start a grocery list. Much of the frustration of waiting is gone if you don't feel it was a total waste of time.

Reading

I am a visually-oriented person. I work as a word monger. In moments of desperation I have been known to read cereal boxes. I can get preachy about the evils of the electronic media—I could read forever. But even something as positive as reading can be a time waster if it is done instead of the planned project.

Sandy reported that unscheduled reading was her downfall, "I'll get involved in a book that I picked up in the process of dusting a room. The book gets finished."

Carol agreed with this problem, "I'll run for the mailbox at work and start to read through all the magazines. On Saturday morning I'll read the newspaper too long. I'll see a new book and think I have to start it right now."

I use reading as a reward when I am finished with a project. Other times when I need a break I will "allow" myself to read for a specified time. Marjorie sets her timer and stops reading when it goes off.

Restricting

When there doesn't seem to be enough time to do a job, give yourself a cushion of time so you are in control. Experts recommend we set personal deadlines so that we're restricting time.

Resumé

Keep track of any information you might need for a resumé rather than waiting for an unexpected entry into the work force or a career change. Record community service projects, correspondence courses, volunteer work and jobs you have held. Keep track of complete dates, names and addresses. Dixie learned this the hard way when she unexpectedly applied for a job and had to search and struggle to remember essential information for her resum that she hadn't recorded.

Simplify

When our boys were younger we simplified their bedrooms. Lots of shelves and sturdy toy boxes helped with clutter. When they were using hard-to-make bunk beds, I bought a patterned fitted sheet to cover the mattress. With a matching slumber bag and pillowcase their beds were stylish, coordinated, and the boys could easily and quickly make them.

Spring Cleaning

From the inventory list I keep in my household notebook I make up a spring cleaning list. It is a very satisfying feeling to have everything in order at one time.

Declare one weekend for this cleaning event and have it be a family project or clear a week on a calendar and do your cleaning. If you are working outside the home and don't have a bulk of time take one item or clean one room on the list at a time and keep on working down the list until everything is finished.

Telephone

I have never decided if the telephone is the boon or the bane of my existence. There are a few tricks that work in getting control over this time-assuming device.

Karen loves her answering machine. When I really need to be left alone I unplug the phone in my office.

When I plan my day I list all the phone calls (with their numbers) that I'm supposed to make. I also write what needs to be covered when I'm on the phone.

> Person to call: Dr. Smith
> Number: 333-3333
> Best Time: 2:00-3:00 P.M.
> Questions: How much longer to give medicine? What did the lab test show?

One of Becky's therapists had a business card made up with the day and times he is available for phone calls. My friends know what time I usually write and try not to call during those hours.

In an interview Ted Engstrom said that we don't have to be available to everyone all the time. Good management lets people know when we're available.

Travel

If you travel frequently try to keep basic travel items packed and ready. I'm always on the look out for sample-sized items. They're a handy and inexpensive way to stock travel items. Have a travel kit of cosmetics and personal items that can stay packed.

Umbrellas and Buggywhips

Go through your house and apply the ole one year test. Be ruthless!

Valentines

You want to send Jane a birthday card but the baby has been sick and you haven't been able to pick up a card. Ever happen to you? Buy an assortment of greeting cards and cover a large shoe box or use an accordion folder. File greeting cards by occasion and keep a good supply.

Waiting

Experts estimate that we spend 10 percent of our lives waiting. I'm sure most women find that a conservative estimate.

Jesus used His waiting time wisely: He talked to the Samaritan woman while getting a drink, taught Mary while Martha was preparing the meal, took a nap while on a boat crossing the water.

Washing

Karen has color-coded baskets for her children. Each child puts his or her dirty laundry in a particular basket and puts it in the laundry area. When the laundry is done, each child is to retrieve his or her basket and put the clean clothes away.

X-rays

Keep track of all family innoculations, X-rays, prescriptions and medical tests. Have a filing system for home medical records.

Xtra Time

Dr. Mark Porter asks,

> Have you found extra time? If you save even 30 minutes a day you will add the equivalent of eleven 16 hour days to your life every year. At this rate, those who are 40 will add one full year to their lives.[8]

Yesterday

> Yesterday is a cancelled check
> Tomorrow is a promissory note
> Today is ready cash. Use it!
>
> —Anonymous

Zinc Oxide

Go through your medicine cabinets and check the expiration dates on all medical supplies and prescriptions. Old medication can be hazardous to your health! Also check for safety, making sure the child-proof caps are properly in place and out of the reach of young, unknowing hands.

Zombie

Don't go through life like a zonked zombie, burned out from overwork. Strive for a balanced life: time for family and friends, time for yourself, time for exercise and leisure, and time with your Creator.

Prayer of Application

Lord,

Thank you for the many lessons learned and for the relevancy of your wise use of time while here during your earthly ministry.

We have covered so much material. Now comes the difficult—but exciting—part of applying it all to our lives. Help us to remember that lasting change takes place one minute, one morning, one day at a time. Help us apply wisely, Lord.

Help us to remember in the hustle and bustle of our fast lane lives that BEING is more important than doing—

—That our time—your time—is not just for spending, but for investing. Help us to invest wisely, Lord.

Amen.

Notes

Chapter 1

1. From *American Couples: Money, Work, and Sex* by Philip Blumstein and Pepper Schwartz. © Copyright 1983, William Morrow & Company, Inc., New York, NY 10016. Used by permission.

2. From MAKING IT TOGETHER AS A TWO-CAREER COUPLE by Marjorie Hansen Shaevitz and Morton H. Shaevitz. Copyright © 1979 by Marjorie Hansen Shaevitz and Morton H. Shaevitz. Reprinted by permission of Houghton Mifflin Company.

3. Anne Follis, "Special Report on Christian Women in America," *Today's Christian Woman* (Fall 1982), p. 67. Used by permission.

4. Blumstein and Schwartz, *American Couples,* p. 28. Used by permission.

5. *Parade Magazine* (May 27, 1984), p. 16.

6. Anne Follis, "Special Report on Christian Women in America," *Today's Christian Woman* (Fall 1982), p. 67. Used by permission.

7. Barbara Kaye Greenleaf with Lewis A. Schaffer, M.D., *Help: A Handbook for Working Mothers* (New York: Thomas Y. Crowell/Berkeley Edition, 1980), p. 55.

8. Ibid.

9. "The Working Wife, Tops in Stress," *Sacramento Bee: Sunday Woman* (October 24, 1981), pp. 8-9.

10. Greenleaf and Schaffer, *Help: A Handbook for Working Mothers,* p. 125.

11. Louis Moore and Kay Moore, *When You Both Go to Work* (Waco, TX: Word Books, 1982), p. 146.

12. "American Women Today," *Ladies Home Journal* (Febraury, 1984).

Chapter 2

1. Rev. Ben Patterson, "Do You Have the Time?" *Leadership* (Spring Quarter, 1982), pp. 50-51. Used by permission.

2. Rev. Wesley Jeske, Fremont Neighborhood Church (January 16, 1977).

3. Taken from MANAGING YOUR TIME, by Ted W. Engstrom and R. Alec MacKenzie. Copyright © 1967 by Zondervan Publishing Huose. Used by permission.

4. Victor Adrian, "Stewardship," *Decision* magazine, October, 1982; © copyright 1982 Billy Graham Evangelistic Association. All rights reserved. Used by permission.

5. Veninga and Spradley, *The Work-Stress Connection,* p. 28.

6. Ruth Senter, "Over the Edge," *Today's Christian Woman* (Spring 1983), p. 74.

7. *Living with Stress* by Lloyd H. Ahlem. © Copyright 1978, Regal Books, Ventura, CA 93006. Used by permission.

8. *Bostonia* magazine, "Stress: What Can Be Done?" Volume 56, December 1982, p. 18. Used by permission.

9. TAKING CHARGE by Gordon McMinn with Larry Libby © 1980, Accent Publications, Inc., Denver, CO. Used by permission.

10. Veninga and Spradley, *The Work-Stress Connection,* p. 90.

11. Ahlem, *Living with Stress,* p. 145. Used by permission.

12. *Spotlight on Stress* by Gary R. Collins. © Copyright 1982, Vision House, Ventura, CA 93006. Used by permission.

13. "Get the Best of Stress," *Athletes in Action* (Spring 1983), p. 17.

Chapter 10

1. ADVENTURES IN PRAYER; Copyright © 1975 by Catherine Marshall. Used by permission of Chosen Books, Lincoln, VA.

2. From the book, MAKING TIME, MAKING MONEY, copyright © 1982 by Rita Davenport. Reprinted with permission of St. Martin's Press, Inc., New York. All rights reserved.

3. From SEEDS OF GREATNESS by Denis Waitley, Copyright © 1983 by Denis E Waitley Inc. Published by Fleming H. Revell Company. Used by permission.

4. Ibid., p. 45. Used by permission.

5. Rita Davenport, *Making Time, Making Money,* p. 160. Reprinted with permission.

Chapter 11

1. Dorothea J. Cudaback, *Human Relations,* U.C. Cooperative Extension, Vol. V, No. 5 (May 1980), p. 1. Used by permission.

2. Barbara Kaye Greenleaf and Lewis A. Schaffer, *Help: A Handbook for Working Mothers* (New York: Thomas Y. Crowell/Berkeley Edition, 1980), p. 262.

3. "When Homemaking Becomes Job 32," *New York Times* (July 14, 1979).

4. Greenleaf and Schaffer, *Help: A Handbook for Working Mothers,* p. 258.
5. Howard Hendricks, *Hendricks on Management* tape series (Ventura, CA: Vision House, n.d.). Used by permission.

6. Ruth Senter, "Over the Edge," *Today's Christian Woman* (Spring 1983), p. 75.

7. Reprinted by permission from WORK, PLAY AND WORSHIP IN A LEISURE-ORIENTED SOCIETY by Gordon Dahl. Copyright Augsburg Publishing House.

8. Charles R. Swindoll, *Strengthening Your Grip,* copyright © 1982, p. 161; used by permission of Word Books, Publisher, Waco, Texas 76796.

9. Maggie Strong, "More Power to You," *Redbook* (September 1983), p. 74.

10. Ruth Senter, "Over the Edge," p. 74.

11. Charles R. Swindoll, *Strengthening Your Grip: Bible Study Guide* (Fullerton, CA: Insight for Living, 1981), pp. 21-22.

Chapter 12

1. Mel White, *Deceived* (Old Tappan, NJ: Fleming H. Revell, 1979), pp. 78-79.

Chapter 13

1. *Strategy for Living* by Edward R. Dayton and Ted W. Engstrom. © Copyright 1976, Regal Books, Ventura, CA 93006. Used by permission.

2. TAKING CHARGE by Gordon McMinn with Larry Libby © 1980, Accent Publications, Inc., Denver, CO. Used by permission.

3. Beverly Stephen, "Discovering the Secret of Success," *Sacramento Bee* (September 19, 1982).

4. Gaily Sheehy, *Pathfinders* (New York: Bantam Books, 1981), p. 15.

4. From A STRATEGY FOR DAILY LIVING by Ari Kiev, M.D. New York: The Free Press, a Division of Macmillan, Inc., 1978. Used by permission.

6. Taken from DISCOVER YOUR POSSIBILITIES, Copyright © 1979 Harvest House PUblishers, 1075 Arrowsmith, Eugene, OR 97402. Used by permission.

7. Dr. Mark Lee, *How to Set Goals* (Portland: Horizon House, 1978), p. 14.

8. Mildred Newman and Bernard Berkowitz, *How to Take Charge of Your Life* (New York: Bantam Books, 1978), p. 15.

Chapter 14

1. *Bostonia* (December 1982), p. 22.

Chapter 15

1. Pat King, *How Do You Find the Time?* (Lynnwood, WA: Aglow, 1975), p. 61. Used by permission.

2. *Bostonia* magazine, "Stress: What Can Be Done?" Volume 56, Numbers 4 & 5, December, 1982, p. 22. Used by permisson.

3. Gloria Gaither, *Decisions* (Waco, TX: Word Boosk, 1982), p. 148.

4. Edward R. Dayton and Ted W. Engstrom, *Strategy for Living.* © Copyright 1976, Regal Books, Ventura, CA 93006. Used by permission.

5. Ted W. Engstrom and Edward R. Dayton, *Strategy for Living,* pp. 67-69. Used by permission.

6. This selection is taken from *Beyond the Kitchen Sink* by Robin Worthington. Copyright, 1979, St. Anthony Messenger Press, 1615 Republic Street, Cincinnati, OH 45210. All rights reserved. Used by permission.

Chapter 16

1. Gloria Gaither, *Decisions* (Waco, TX: Word Books, 1982), p. 27.

2. Dorothea J. Cudaback, *Human Relations,* U.C. Cooperative Extension, Vol. V, No. 6 (June 1980), p. 6. Used by permission.

3. Taken from STRESS IN THE FAMILY, Copyright © 1982 Harvest House Publishers, 1075 Arrowsmith, Eugene, OR 97402. Used by permission.

4. Taken from GOD'S WILL FOR YOUR LIFE, Copyright © 1982 Harvest House Publishers, 1075 Arrowsmith, Eugene, OR 97402. Used by permission.

5. Gloria Gaither, *Decisions,* p. 73.

Chapter 17

1. Douglas J. Rumford, "How to Say No Graciously," *Leadership* (Fall 1982), p. 93. Used by permission.

2. *If Being a Christian Is So Great, Why Do I Have the Blahs?* by John Dobbert. © Copyright 1980, Regal Books, Ventura, CA 93006. Used by permission.

3. Ibid., p. 125. Used by permission.

4. D. G. Kehl, "Burnout: The Risk of Reaching Too High," *Christianity Today,* November 20, 1981, p. 28. Used by permission.

5. Edward C. Bliss, *Getting Things Done* (New York: Bantam Books, 1976), p. 100.

6. Lloyd Ogilvie, *The Bush Is Still Burning* (Waco, TX: Word Books, 1980), p. 9.

7. Howard Hendricks, *Hendricks on Management* tape series (Ventura, CA: Vision House, N.D.). Used by permission.

8. *Spotlight on Stress* by Gary R. Collins. © Copyright 1982, Vision House, Ventura, CA 93006. Used by permission.

9. Anne Ortlund, *The Disciplines of the Beautiful Woman* (Waco, TX: Word Books, 1977), p. 52.

10. "Yes to Something Higher" by Gloria Gaither. © Copyright 1978 by William J. Gaither. All rights reserved. Used by permission of Gaither Music Company.

Chapter 18

1. Reprinted by permission from THE CREATIVE HOMEMAKER by Mary Bouma, published and copyright 1973, Bethany House Publishers, Minneapolis, Minnesota 55438.

2. Stephen Douglas, *Managing Yourself* (San Bernardino, CA: Here's Life Publishers, 1978), p. 31.

3. "An Interview with Ed Dayton," *Leadership* (Spring 1982), p. 16.

4. Jay E. Adams, *You Can Conquer Depression* (Grand Rapids: Baker Book House, 1975), p. 15. Used by permission.

5. Charles Shedd, *Time for All Things* (Nashville: Abingdon, 1962), p. 92. Used by permission.

6. Harold H. LeCrone, Jr., "Coping with Stress." Reprinted by permission from CHRISTIAN LIFE magazine, copyright May 1983, Christian Life Missions, 396 E. St. Charles Rd., Wheaton, IL 60188.

7. Susan Issacs, "All in a Day's Work—Four Women's Stories," *Parents* (December 1982), p. 51.

8. Stephen Douglas, *Managing Yourself*, p. 57.

Chapter 19

1. Taken from HOW TO HANDLE PRESSURE by Clyde and Ruth Narramore. Published by Tyndale House Publishers, Inc., © 1975. Used by permission.

Martha's Time-Saver Primer

1. FROM: WHAT WIVES WITH THEIR HUSBANDS KNEW ABOUT WOMEN, by Dr. James Dobson. Published by Tyndale House Publishers, Inc. © 1975. Used by permission.

2. This selection is taken from *Beyond the Kitchen Sink* by Robin

Worthington. Copyright 1979, St. Anthony Messenger Press, 1615 Republic Street, Cincinnati, OH 45210. All rights reserved. Used by permission.

3. Edward C. Bliss, *Getting Things Done* (New York: Bantam Books, 1976), p. 124.

4. Mary Beth Moster, *When Mom Goes to Work* (Chicago: Moody Press, 1980), p. 107. Used by permission.

5. From MAKING TIME WORK FOR YOU by Harold J. Taylor. Reprinted by permission of General Publishing Co. Limited, Toronto, Canada.

6. From the book, KILLING GIANTS PULLING THORNS by Charles R. Swindoll, copyright 1978 by Charles R. Swindoll. Published by Multnomah Press, Portland, Oregon 97266. Used by permission.

7. Dr. Mark Porter, *The Times of Your Life* (Wheaton, IL: Victor Books, 1983), p. 122. Used by permission.

Bibliography

Ahlem, Lloyd H. *Living With Stress.* Ventura, CA: Regal Books, 1978.

Angus, Fay. *Up to Heaven and Down to Earth.* Ventura, CA: Regal Books, 1977.

Anson, Elva and Linden, Kathie. *The Compleat Family Book.* Chicago: Moody Press, 1979.

Barnes, Emilie. *More Hours in my Day.* Eugene, OR: Harvest House, 1982.

Bliss, Edwin C. *Doing It Now: A Twelve-Step Program for Curing Procrastination and Achieving Your Goals.* New York: Scribner, 1983.

——————. *Getting Things Done.* New York: Bantam, 1976.

Bombeck, Erma. *Aunt Erma's Cope Book.* New York: Fawcett Crest, 1979.

Bouma, Mary L. *The Creative Homemaker.* Minneapolis: Bethany House, 1973.

Bowman, George M. *Clock Wise.* Old Tappan, NJ: Fleming H. Revell, 1979.

Brace, Pam and Jones, Peggy. *Sidetracked Home Executives.* Portland, OR: Binford and Mort, 1977.

Collins, Gary R. *Spotlight on Stress.* Ventura, CA: Vision House, 1977.

Conran, Shirley. *Superwoman.* New York: Bantam, 1978.

Dahl, Gordon. *Work, Play and Worship in a Leisure-Oriented Society.* Minneapolis: Augsburg Publishing House, 1972.

Davenport, Rita. *Making Time, Making Money: A Step-By-Step Program to Set Your Goals and Achieve Success.* New York: St. Martin's Press, 1982.

Dayton, Edward R., and Engstrom, Ted W. *Stragegy for Living: How to Make the Best of Your Time and Abilities.* Ventura, CA: Regal Books, 1976.

Dayton, Edward R. *Tools for Time Management: Time-Saving Tools for Managing Your Life.* Grand Rapids, MI: Zondervan, 1974.

Dobbert, John. *If Being a Christian Is So Great Why Do I Have the Blahs?* Ventura, CA: Regal Books, 1980.

Doonebal, Baukje and Lemstra, Tjitske. *Homemaking.* Colorado Springs: NavPress, 1981.

Douglas, Stephen B. *Managing Yourself.* San Bernardino, CA: Here's Life Publishers, 1978.

Engstrom, Ted W., and Dayton, Edward R. *The Act of Management for Christian Leaders.* Waco, TX: Word, 1982.

Engstrom, Ted W., and MacKenzie, R. Alec. *Managing Your Time.* Grand

Rapids, MI: Zondervan, 1967.

Engstrom, Ted W. *The Pursuit of Excellence*. Grand Rapids, MI: Zondervan, 1982.

Gaither, Gloria. *Decisions: A Christian's Guide to Making Right Choices*. Waco, TX: Word, 1982.

Gault, Jan L. *Free Time: Making Your Leisure Count*. New York: Wiley, 1982.

Gilbert, Lela. *Just Five Days Till Friday*. Denver: Accent Books, 1979.

Greenleaf, Barbara Kaye with Schaffer, M.D., Lewis A. *Help: A Handbook for Working Mothers*. New York: Berkeley, 1979.

Hansel, Tim. *When I Relax I Feel Guilty*. Elgin, IL: David C. Cook, 1979.

Hendricks, Howard. *Hendricks on Management*, tape series. Ventura, CA: Vision House, N.D.

Hensley, Dennis E. *Positive Workaholism: Making the Most of Your Time*. Indianapolis: R & R Newkirk, 1983.

_____. *Staying Ahead of Time*. Indianapolis: R & R Newkirk, 1981.

Herr, Ethel. *Chosen Women of the Bible*. Chicago: Moody Press, 1976.

Hummel, Charles E. *Tyranny of the Urgent*. Downers Grove, IL: Inter-Varsity Press, 1967.

Hunt, Gladys. *Ms. Means Myself*. Grand Rapids, MI: Zondervan, 1972.

Hunter, Brenda. *Where Have All the Mothers Gone?* Grand Rapids, MI: Zondervan, 1982.

King, Pat. *How Do You Find the Time?* Lynnwood, WA: Aglow Publications, 1975.

LaHaye, Tim. *How to Manage Pressure Before Pressure Manages You*. Grand Rapids, MI: Zondervan, 1983.

_____. *How to Win Over Depression*. Grand Rapids, MI: Zondervan, 1974.

Lakein, Alan. *How To Get Control of Your Time and Your Life*. New York: Signet Books, 1973.

Landorf, Joyce. *I Came to Love You Late*. Old Tappan, NJ: Fleming H. Revell, 1977.

Lee, Mark. *How to Set Goals and Really Reach Them*. Fremont, CA: Horizon Books, 1978.

Le Tourneau, Richard. *Management Plus*. Grand Rapids, MI: Zondervan, 1976.

Littauer, Florence. *The Pursuit of Happiness*. Eugene, OR: Harvest House, 1978.

MacKenzie, Alec and Waldo, Kay Cronkite. *About Time! A Woman's Guide to Time Management*. New York: McGraw-Hill, 1981.

Marshall, Catherine. *Adventures in Prayer.* Lincoln, VA: Chosen Books, 1978.

McBride, Pat. *How to Get Your Act Together When Nobody Gave You the Script.* Nashville: Thomas Nelson, 1982.

McMinn, Gordon and Libby, Larry. *Taking Charge: The Dynamics of Personal Decision-Making and Self-Management.* Denver: Accent Books, 1980.

McQuade, Walter and Aikman, Ann. *Stress.* New York: Bantam, 1974.

Miller, Ruth Wagner. *The Time Minder.* Chappaqua, NY: Christian Herald Books, 1980.

Moore, Louis and Moore, Kay. *When You Both Go to Work.* Waco, TX: Word Books, 1982.

Moster, Mary Beth. *When Mom Goes to Work.* Chicago: Moody Press, 1980.

Murphy, Cecil. *Getting There from Here.* Waco, TX: Word Books, 1981.

Narramore, Bruce. *You're Someone Special.* Grand Rapids, MI: Zondervan, 1978.

Narramore, Clyde and Narramore, Ruth. *How to Handle Pressure.* Wheaton, IL: Tyndale House, 1981.

Newman, Mildred and Berkowitz, Bernard. *How to Take Charge of Your Life.* New York: Bantam, 1978.

Ogilvie, Lloyd John. *The Bush Is Still Burning.* Waco, TX: Word Books, 1980.

—————. *God's Will in Your Life.* Eugene, OR: Harvest House, 1982.

—————. Praying with Power. Ventura, CA: Regal Books, 1984.

Ortlund, Anne. *The Disciplines of the Beautiful Woman.* Waco, TX: Word Books, 1977.

Osgood, Don. *Pressure Points.* Chappaqua, NY: Christian Herald Books, 1978.

Peale, Norman Vincent. *The Power of Positive Thinking.* Old Tappan, NJ: Spire Books, 1952.

Perry, Charles. *Why Christians Burn Out.* Nashville: Thomas Nelson, 1982.

Polston, Ruth Ann. *You Deserve to be Happy.* Eugene, OR: Harvest House, 1978.

Porat, Frieda. *Creative Procrastination: Organizing Your Own Life.* New York: Harper and Row, 1980.

Porter, Mark. *The Time of Your Life.* Wheaton, IL: Victor Books, 1983.

Schuller, Robert H. *Discover Your Possibilities.* Eugene, OR: Harvest House, 1980.

—————. *Turning Your Stress into Strength.* Eugene, OR: Harvest House, 1978.

Sehnert, M.D., Keith. *Stress-Unstress.* Minneapolis: Augsburg, 1981.

Shedd, Charlie W. *Time for All Things.* Nashville: Abingdon, 1962.

Sheehy, Gail. *Pathfinders.* New York: Bantam, 1982.

Sherrow, Jeanne E. *It's About Time: A Look at Leisure, Life-style and Christianity.* Grand Rapids, MI: Zondervan, 1984.

Swindoll, Charles R. *Killing Giants, Pulling Thorns.* Portland, OR: Multnomah, 1978.

——————. *Strengthening Your Grip.* Waco, TX: Word Books, 1982.

——————. *Strengthening Your Grip Bible Study Guide.* Fullerton, CA: Insight for Living, 1981.

Taylor, Harold L. *Making Time Work for You: A Guidebook to Effective and Productive Time Management.* New York: Beaufort Books, 1981.

Timmons, Tim. *Stress in the Family: How to Live Through It.* Eugene, OR: Harvest House, 1982.

Veninga, Robert L., and Spradley, James P. *The Work-Stress Connection: How to Cope with Job Burnout.* New York: Ballentine Books, 1981.

Waitley, Denis. *Seeds of Greatness.* Old Tappan, NJ: Fleming H. Revell, 1983.

Ward, Patricia A. and Stout, Martha. *Christian Women at Work.* Grand Rapids, MI: Zondervan, 1981.

White, Mel. *Deceived.* Old Tappan, NJ: Spire Books, 1979.

Winston, Stephanie. *Getting Organized.* New York: Warner Books, 1978.

Wise, Karen. *Confessions of a Totaled Woman.* Nashville: Thomas Nelson, 1980.

Wise, Robert. *How Not to Go Crazy.* Eugene, OR: Harvest House, 1980.

Worthington, Robin. *Beyond the Kitchen Sink.* Cincinnati: St. Anthony Messenger Press, 1979.

The publisher does not necessarily endorse the entire contents of all publications referred to in this book.

For information in scheduling a time stewardship
workshop please contact:

Bonnie G. Wheeler
P.O. Box 381
Williams, CA 95987